The
Adventures
of my
Life

John Banner

authorHOUSE®

AuthorHouse™
1663 Liberty Drive
Bloomington, IN 47403
www.authorhouse.com
Phone: 1 (800) 839-8640

Published by AuthorHouse 07/08/2020

ISBN: 978-1-7283-6601-2 (sc)
ISBN: 978-1-7283-6602-9 (e)

Library of Congress Control Number: 2020912155

Print information available on the last page.

Contents

Chapter 1   New York 1

Chapter 2   New Jersey 2

Chapter 3   Pennsylvania 3

Chapter 4   Daily Life on the Farm 8

Chapter 5   The Bus 10

Chapter 6   The Schools in Pennsylvania 12

Chapter 7   Middle School 14

Chapter 8   More Middle School 18

Chapter 9   7th Grade 20

Chapter 10 8th Grade 21

Chapter 11 High School 23

Chapter 12 Kentucky 25

Chapter 13 11th Grade 27

Chapter 14 The Partying Days 28

Chapter 15 Concerts 32

Chapter 16 Voc School 34

Chapter 17 12th Grade 35

Chapter 18 Girls in Kentucky 38

Chapter 19 The Class Trip and Graduation 40

Chapter 20 A Return to Elementary School Days 42

Chapter 21 Back to Kentucky for A Minute 44

Chapter 22 Massachusetts 46

Chapter 23   Jobs..48

Chapter 24   More Jobs 56

Chapter 25   Untitled 60

Chapter 26   More Jobs 62

Chapter 27   More Partying Days 64

Chapter 28   My Motorcycle 66

Chapter 29   Mushrooms, and French Girls...........................69

Chapter 30   The Cars II had in My Life 70

Chapter 31   My Conversion to Christ 72

Chapter 32   Holly 75

Chapter 33   Rule and The Day I Quit 79

Chapter 34   Israel 80

Chapter 35   Stupid Dr. Ritzkrak 85

Chapter 36   The Arbor 86

Chapter 37   Agh and Webber II 88

Chapter 38   Danvers State 90

Chapter 39   Webber II Round 2 92

Chapter 40   Danvers State Again 95

Chapter 41   Jesus Continued 97

Chapter 42   Hillcrest 99

Chapter 43   John 101

Chapter 44   The Nova and The Z Car 104

Chapter 45   The Wabbit and The Pathfinder...................... 107

Chapter 46   The Cops and Fred 109

Chapter 47   Apartments 110

Chapter 48   Kevin Hanes 111

Chapter 49   The Heights A Cape Ann................................ 112

Chapter 50   The Fire 114

Chapter 51   Uncle Saul.. 116

Chapter 52   Paul... 118

Chapter 53   Mount Washington 119

Chapter 54   Mount Katadin 120

Chapter 55   Eastern River Expeditions 121

Chapter 56   The Suzuki RM 125 123

Chapter 57   Caleb 124

Chapter 58   The Fire Works... 126

Chapter 59 The Jumping Jehovas 127
Chapter 60 The Fire 128
Chapter 61 The Horses 129
Chapter 62 Matt 130
Chapter 63 The Ring 131
Chapter 64 Bobby Mercury 132
Chapter 65 The Apartment 134
Chapter 66 Emily 136
Chapter 67 Bobby Mercury Again 137
Chapter 68 Martha 138
Chapter 69 The Suicide Attempt 140
Chapter 70 My Experience at Bay Ridge 142
Chapter 71 The Food 145
Chapter 72 Bay Ridge Continued 146
Chapter 73 Bobby Mercury Again 152
Chapter 74 The Laughing Fits 153
Chapter 75 The Blood Guy 155
Chapter 76 The Room 156
Chapter 77 In The Milleau 158
Chapter 78 The Food and the Lady with the Pill 160
Chapter 79 My Visitors 161
Chapter 80 The Last Few Days 163
Chapter 81 The Round Up 165
Chapter 82 The Last Day 166
Chapter 83 Layland Unit Beverly Hospital 167
Chapter 84 The Patients 170
Chapter 85 Tewksbury State Hospital 175
Chapter 86 Wrapping Tewksbury State Hospital 178
Chapter 87 The Respite House 180
Chapter 88 The Staff 183
Chapter 89 The Clients 185
Chapter 90 Leaving the House 186

About the Book

This book will bring you on a thrilling roller coaster ride of sex, drugs, and rock and roll, jobs, cars, Jesus, Christianity, partying, mental health issues, a suicide attempt, and psych hospitalizations.

The book starts with the author's earliest memories, of preschool in New York, living in New Jersey, and moving to Pennsylvania. Our family lived on a farm that we rented. It had an inground swimming pool, and we had farm animals. One night the men were working in the barn, when a guy accidently started a fire by knocking over a trouble light, and catching a small puddle of gasoline on fire. The barn burned down to the ground, the horses escaped, but the chickens got fried. The landlord wanted us out.

So we moved to another farm about 20m meter a way. This farm we owned, the house was built in the 1700's. We had a 13 acre farm, with a huge barn, rolling pastures, a corn crib, a chicken coup, a basketball court, and we built an inground pool. Everyday all the laids from the neighborhood used to come to our house to play in the barn, and the pool.

Life was great on the farm, and then tragedy struck as our parents got divorced. The book falters the story of John and his father moving to Kentucky, and going to school there. During the 11th grade John was introduced to marijuana, and he had friends that used to smoke pot with him at his trailor, while his father was away in trips.

The story follows John's exodus to Massachusetts, to be reunited with his mother, and siblings.

There was a lot of partying in the woods of West Gloucester, every Friday night with beer and pot. There is a lot of motorcycle riding adventures, where John out ran two state troopers on his motorcycle, trying to escape from the law into the woods of West Gloucester, also riding adventures on the back roads, around the reservoir, and pipeline. Even a comical ride right into the ocean on his bike, at night.

The story talks about all the cars John owned, and the various jobs he did. John's sexual affair with his girlfriend, and his conversion into Christ. His trip to Israel and his life lead as onto the Lord.

The story then proceeds with John's mental health problems, and psych hospitalizations visitations. His beautiful apartment at "the fort" and his suicide attempt.

The book then recounts John's seven month commitment to 3 different psych hospitals, a harrowing tale of what goes on in these places, that the outside world has no idea of what goes on there. Then his five month stay at a respite house, and then finally a new apartment and a new start at life in W. Gloucester. Finally ending John's loved for his Lord, who helped him all the time on the hospital, and now to a godly life style.

Chapter 1
New York

I was born in Laredo, TX, at the air force base, my mother and father were both in the military. Starting with my earliest recollection, "we", meaning my father and mother and brother and I, lived in New York. I remember my father had a red MG, and he gave rides to all the neighborhood kids around the block.

I remember going to preschool, where at lunch you ran to the small barn, and tried to grab a "Big Wheel", from the pile of rideable toys. I always seemed to get stuck with the "Inch Worm", a small green toy that you sat on, and by going up and down, it crawled along. The faster kids always got the "Big Wheels" ahead of me.

Chapter 2
New Jersey

Then I remember we moved to New Jersey, where my sister Cathy was born. All the neighborhood teens wanted to push Cathy around in the baby carriage, because she was so beautiful.

One day me and my friend Eddie were jumping on his bed. And Eddie fell and hit his head on the bed post. Blood started coming out and he kicked his feet up and down from the pain. I just started laughing because of the way he was doing it, and I laughed. I couldn't help it, it looked funny and I just laughed.

One day we had a cardboard box from a new appliance in the yard, and all the kids were playing in it. But I had to go to bed early each night. All the kids were still out playing in our yard, and I was in bed. I hated my mother for that. But I got over it.

Chapter 3

Pennsylvania

Next we moved to a farm in Pennsylvania. It was a nice house with a big barn, and a garage. There was also an inground swimming pool there. When all the men were done working in garage, with their cars, they jumped in the pool, and all the ladies said "we need to throw in a bar of soap for you to get rid of all that grease on your arms.

One day me and my friend Cindy Barker were swimming, and I was underwater and Cindy was there too, and I accidently kicked her with my foot in the eye. And she was in the water in pain. I felt so sorry. We had a big tent in the backyard. It was actually a parachute tent, like a small circus tent. And me and Cindy were on the cot kissing. And my father saw it and broke us up. You would have thought he would congratulate me for scoring, but no.

Next there was a goat standing on the hood of my fathers Datsun 240 Z car. He had a gun where were at, by the pool, and he threatened to kill it. But my mother cried "don't shoot it" and he didn't. It was funny to see that goat on the hood of the car.

Another animal adventure I remember was we had roosters. And at supper time we fed them from dog bowls. And the freaking rooster attacked me. It about scared me to death. It's wings were flapping and his beak pecking at me. Like I said, I was scared.

One night me and my brother, Chris, were in our room sleeping, and my brother said to me, John the barn's on fire. But I didn't believe him and I went to sleep. The guys were working in the garage, and one guy accidently threw a trouble light into a small puddle of gas/oil mix. There was a spark, then there was a fire. The barn burned down, the horses escaped into the field, but the chickens got fried. Needless to say the landlord wanted us out.

Next we moved to another farm in the rurals of Coopersburg. The house was awesome. It was built in the 1700's. Four floors, six staircases, five bedrooms, two bathrooms, kitchen, dining room, living room, den, a hallway for a second door, a laundry room, an attic, and two sides of the basement. One side of the basement was made into a family room, with a dry bar, four swivel stools for the bar, an octagonal table with four swivel chairs for it, and one of three fireplaces.

One day me and my brother, moved the couch to the heater, with a blanket over it to keep the heat in. We tried to watch Saturday morning cartoons there. We lit a fire one day, but the flu was closed, and my friend Danny reached in the chimney while the fire was burning, and opened the flu, just in the nick of time, because that would have been a disaster, with all the smoke not being able to escape.

The farm was 13 acres. We had a medium sized backyard, with an inground pool, 41'ft, x 18'ft. at the Widest point. The pool was shaped like a kidney, with a diving board, and ladder, 8'ft. deep. There was another yard to the side of the pool. It contained a cherry tree. All my friends used to pick the cherry's off and throw them at each other. The cherry's used to go in the pool, and we would dive down to the bottom and get them out.

There was a pool house with all the chlorine, and water testers. There were lights along the side of the pool, and a small concrete area, by the shallow end, for lounging and peppered with shrubs on one side for privacy. I learned how to clean the pool with its vacuum cleaner.

There was a huge barn, with a green roll roof. My father made a carport on one side of an extension to the barn. He was into collecting old cars. There was a garage with a concrete floor, and a pit in the middle, so you could work on the undersides of cars. Inside the barn was 4 stalls. One stall had an automatic water bowl, the horses (we had a lot of) would push there noses into the little lever that allowed the water to come out automatically. We had to get the manure out of one stall once, and we had a blast removing the manure with wheel barrows. Saying "this is the captain speaking, we are expecting turdulance".

The main floor of the barn was for storing hay. There was 2 sides of the bales of hay, that we used to build hay forts. Every kid in the neighborhood would come to our farm to play, all summer long.

We built hay forts,., and played cops and robbers with realistic toy gun, we played hide and go seek with rules that you couldn't go into any of the antique cars, or in the garage. Then we used to jump off the ladder that led up to the high beams, about 30'ft. up into the loose hay. I never used to climb to the very top beam, because you would have to balance yourself, and I was afraid to jump off from the tallest beam.

There was also a burnt out building. All that was left of it was its burnt wall of wooden boards. It had a concrete floor, and we installed a basketball rim, with its backboard. My 3 friends painted the Celtics on the floor, and N.O. Jazz on the other side of the court. We made a nice court, but we never played a single game, there. We did used to play horse though. That was fun. I used to make shots, bending over backwards.

There was also a corn crib. It contained 2 sides, fenced in with corn on the cob, for feeding horses, and cows. My father rented the corn crib out to a neighbor with their corn. On the top floor was a conveyor belt for moving the corn. There were pigeon nests in the belt. We used to have huge corn fights. My brother and his friends on one side, and me and my friends on the other. We shucked the kernels into 5 gallon buckets, until it was full. Then we threw the corn at each other. It was really fun.

There was a electric line tower in the pasture, a high tension wire tower. I climbed up it one day and was getting close to the wires. Then I decided to climb down before I fried myself.

The farm had 3 fields for horses and cows. One field had a great hill for sledding. We had many horses. One was named Sarge, a Tennessee walker. I tried to ride him one day, and got bucked off. I got right back on him, just like the parable says, 'If you get bucked off a horse get right back on him. There was also Yoo Hoo Roo, an appaliasion. He was a barrel racer, I rode him and he would turn on a dime, when you laid a reign on his neck. You really had to hold on because, forward inertia of the gallup to the turn, you could easily fall off. My father got this horse from a black man at his air national guard base, in willow grove. The name Yoo Hoo Roo is swaheliy for freedom.

One day Sarge was jealous at a new baby horse we had, and he ran into death. We had cows. We all had our own cows, John cow, Chris cow, my brother, and Cathy cow, my sister. The deal was that we would all feed the cows, and raise them, and when it was time for them to be sold, we would get a motorcycle from my father. I was the only one who got a motorcycle. It was originally a Kawasaki 125, but my father bought me a KE 100 instead. It used to suck feeding the cows before school started each day. There was a bucket with a nipple on it. And I used to feed my cow each day, with powdered milk. I couldn't feed the cow hardly because, each time I would lower the bucket over the railing, the stupid cow would butt its head against the bucket, and spill the milk.

Another field had a sheep pasture. And there was Lammy Pie. A male sheep with balls, like soft balls, hanging down. All my friends would run around and take cover by a piece of farm equipment, because Lammy would butt you. The farm machine was your only safety.

We had pigs, that we kept in one stall, and fed them handsomely with food from a neighbor friend of my father's. The neighbor worked at a supermarket, and he would get spoiled food from the store to feed the pigs. Another friend of my father's got in on the deal too, with his pig. We feed them and when they were all fattened up. They went to the butcher, every body got free bacon, sausage, ham, and pork.

There was chickens too. We had a chicken catcher, that was fun to use to catch chickens Its just a metal rod, with a hook on the end, that you would gaff the wandering chicken by the leg. One day a banana spider spun a web across the path to the chicken coop. It was menacing. One day mosquitos, stung my brother in the chest. I laughed because I thought it was funny. I was kind of mean to Chris. I think God punished me for laughing by giving me big nipples. That was always an embarrassment for me. (More on that later.)

We had a fenced in garden. And a narrow creek with fresh water, that lead to a small pond. From there the pond water flowed down to another narrow creek, to the corner of the property downhill. One day my brother and I played at the pond. We stood at each side of the pond, and threw rocks at the opposite shore. The mud would splash all over you.

We also had goats. One goat tried to jump over the fence. But didn't jump high enough, and her milk bag ripped open and got caught in the barb wired fence. We had to call the vet.

Chapter 4
Daily Life on the Farm

All the kids in the neighborhood came to our house. It was the place to be. All day we played in the hot barn, in the hay bales, making hay forts. Then at night we all swam in the pool.

In the pool we would have one kid in the water, then the rest of us would dive off the diving board one at a time in a row, to see how long the kid in the water, could take the constant water bombardment. Then when he couldn't take it anymore, someone else would tread water and be splashed.

Me and my sister Cathy would play submarine. I was the submarine and Cathy rode on my back, as we swam side to side under water.

One of my father's friends had a giant life raft, military style. We used to swim under it, and then stick our heads under the raft where there was a pocket of air. We just jumped on that thing till it finally ripped.

My father's friend John Smith, gave me a dollar if I could swim the length of the pool, underwater. I swam the distance no problem and received the dollar.

In the backyard we played football, and baseball. It seemed like me and my brother were always on opposite teams. He had his friends, and I had mine. I always beat him playing football. My father said "Let him win", but I never did I always beat him.

On my team was Danny Hunter. He was a great friend of mine. He was the quarterback, and I was the runner, and wide receiver. We had a special connection, as every ball he threw I caught for touchdowns. We played against the Appleton brothers, Steve, and Bob. Steve was afraid to tackle. He used to hike his leg up so he wouldn't get hurt. Me and Danny played one game at their house. I had a 100 yard game running that day.

We had a dog named Ruffies. Ruffies understood the game of football. He used to make tackles. We called him the all time interferer. Finally we had to make a rule, anything that Ruffies does counts. Me and Ruffies used to wrestle each other.

We used to play baseball, and kickball too. One day I was up to bat, and my dog Patches, a Jordan setter, was standing there. And I swung the bat at the ball, and I accidently hit Patches right in the eye. He let out a yelp, and I blinded him. I felt so sorry. It was a total accident but I felt bad.

In the house which was white with stucco, and yellow alumin siding, with black shutters, we played tag. It was running up and down the stairs, and running through the hallway. I never got tagged. We threw stuffed animals at each other. We played hide and seek at night in the yard. We had rules that you couldn't go in the barn, but anywhere else. We did one potato, two potato, to find out who was it. Then when the kid counted to 100, we ran off in 10 different directions. The deal was that the last kid caught was it for the next round. This made it you wanted to get home base as soon as you can and not get caught.

We also had a tree house. Once again we built mine and then we built Chris' house. We never finished it. Just the two floors.

So I was an alter boy at the episcopal church in Quakertown. I used to carry the cross, and snuff out the candles. It was fun. We went to see the Jesus film as a church. I went to confirmation classes there and the bishop laid hands on me and I think the Holy Spirit moved on me.

My father used to buzz the house in his air national guard plane, an 02. It was a duel propeller plane with one prop that pulled and one prop that pushes. We would be in the back yard playing football, and my father buzzed the house. As he left he would always dip the wings from side to side to say bye-bye. I was so proud of my dad.

Chapter 5
The Bus

I was always late for the bus. I had to run up the driveway as fast as I could to get on the waiting bus. The bus driver was Ernie Bird. She was mean. One day I was sitting in the front of the bus, and I crumbled a piece of paper in a ball. Then I took up a shot, and threw it at a five gallon bucket for trash. The shot missed the bucket, and Ernie Bird said I was littering, and wanted me to write "I will not throw paper on the bus a 100x. There was no way I was going to write 'I will not throw paper on the bus' not throw paper on the bus" 100x, when all I did was take up a shot and missed it. So she kicked me off the bus, and I had to ride to school by our house sitter. (More on that later,).

There were two busses that went by my stop. It was embarrassing, I had to stand there as one bus went by, before my bus came.

On the bus, I liked to sit in the back of the bus with all the cool kids. But I was bullied by the Annette brothers, and Bob Appleton. That was in the morning. On the ride home from school there was this idiot who bullied me and my friend Lorne. Everyday he would sit beside me and say "do you have your football uniform on?" Then he would say "do you have your helmet on?" And he would hit me in the head. Then he would say "do you have your shoulder pads on?" And he would hit me in the shoulder. And then he would say "do you have your thigh pads on?" And he would hit me in the thigh. And then he would say 'do you have your knee pads on?' And he would hit me in the knee.

Everyday it was the same thing. He would give us massive beatings. So finally I said to my friend Lorne, who got hit too, "let's get this guy". The two of us together can beat this guy. But Lorne didn't want to do it. So everyday the massive beatings continued.

Then the kids used to make fun of my brother. They used to call him "chipmunk cheeks". Because his cheeks flared out because of the medicine he was taking. And I said to Chris, I'm sorry there is nothing I can do". All these kids were bigger and meaner than me.

But one day, our bus driver, a cool guy, also used to drive school bus for kids at Perkisee. So we wanted to play football against the kids at the other school. We set it up to meet their team, about only three of them showed up. So we split our guys and gave them players, to play.

I caught a difficult pass that seemed to float right into my hands, for a touchdown, in traffic. The next day they posted the score on a sign in the front of the bus. The sign said we won' with surprise touchdown catch by John (p.f.) peach fuzz, Banner, I was embarrassed a little.

Chapter 6

The Schools in Pennsylvania

I went to Lower Milford Elementary school in second grade. Lunch was always my favorite part of the day. I used to load up on ice cream. We played kickball at recess. Fourth grade was the last year for the teacher, before she retired. We were lucky to have her as teacher. Fifth grade was Mr. Leeser.

One day the fifth and second grade students switched classes. I had to do second grade math, and I got a lot of answers wrong, and they were concerned. Another friend of mine had wrong answers too. Mr. Leeser pointed to the lockers, and had us line up. He said "you got a lot of answers wrong in second grade math," and my friend said "oh, I was just trying to be funny." And I thought that was a good answer, so I said "I was just trying to be funny too." And I got away with it. In the fifth grade, we all had knicknames, from the tv shows, Happy Days, and Welcome Back Kotter. I was Potsy.

We had a trail through the woods, behind the school for the fifth graders. It was a nature trail, and we identified many trees, and birds. In one section of the woods we set up bird feeders. I brought some scrapple from the pigs we had on the farm to put out.

But I missed field day. Me and my friend Gene Cavanaugh, were going to do the wheelbarrow race. I was speedy as the wheelbarrow. We probably would have won first place in the event, but for some reason I decided to pretend I was sick and I stayed home from field day. It seemed like every major point in my life I backed out of.

(More to follow). How stupid of me.

Chapter 7
Middle School

Middle school was cool. They put you in houses according to how smart you were. We were 6G, and called ourselves the gazelles, for field day, because gazelles are fast. Gym class was cool. They had us do gymnastics. I was good on the balance beam, and the horse. We played with a giant rubber ball, that we kicked around in crab leg position. Me and my friend were the goalies. It was a very low scoring game.

One day after gym class, me and my friend Gary Bolt, skipped the rest of the day. We snuck past the windows below the glass, so no one could see us. We finally made a break for it and we walked all the way to his house. About 10 miles. Then we played basketball. I suck at basketball.

While in elementary and middle school, we went to many foreign countries. My father was a commercial airline pilot for TWA. So we flew everywhere for free. Our first trip we went to Greece. All I remember was Mt. Acropolis, and the Parthenon. Just an ancient temple. I took pictures of this Greek god who was naked. And a security guard said I was not allowed to take photos.

We travelled to the island of Crete. On the return trip to the mainland, we couldn't get on a flight. We travelled standby, and plane after plane after plane went without us. We were their many hours and finally caught a plane back to Greece.

While in Greece, we went on a cruise ship. The waves were severe and the ship was rocking in the curent. Me and this other kid were standing on the bow, and the ship was bouncing and each wave caused the ship to dive and rise. Me and the other kid were leaving our feet as the ship cruised along. So Chris thought he would jump too, and was rising as the ship rose and fell. Finally the captain came up to us and said we couldn't jump no more, and he broke us up.

My family and I went to Italy. All I remember was it took hours to get from the airport to Rome. I remember the collosium, and a statue of a god. We had real pasta at a restaurant, but I didn't like it. Then we went to the Vatican, but did not see the pope.

We went to Portugal. I remember we were at a restaurant and there was a teenager next to us drinking wine. And I was jealous, and wanted my father to give me some wine too. But he said I was too young. As the dancers danced around around the tables, you threw plates at their feet, and they would smash into pieces. Later on we went back to the hotel and the teenager came too. He was an actor and had a small role in the film "The Boys From Brazil". Me, my brother, and the teenager were standing on the deck of the hotel room about 20 stories up, we contemplated on to spit on people or not. We didn't.

We drove around to a cliff. The locals would hang on to railings on the side of the cliff and go to the bathroom.

Then we went to Ireland. We drove a rental mini, and picked up an old goat farmer hitchhiker. There was barely enough room for the five of us. Now we had to pick up this guy. When he got in the car, we couldn't understand him because his gaelick accent was so thick. He smelled like goats, and I was glad to get rid of him.

Then we went to Blarney Castle, and I kissed the blarney stone. You have to get on your back and grab the railing, and tilt your head back to kiss the stone. Its supposed to give you the gift of gab, but I didn't say much after that.

Next we went to El Salvador. We went to some waterfall basin of water next and swam around in the water and Chris took off. We found him a little while later. We drove off to the northern part of the country and got a room for the night. We didn't know that a little farther up was a much nicer hotel. My father felt bad and made it up to the innkeeper by having dinner at their hotel in an outside seating area that had hammocks in the trees.

We went to a local beach, and picked up some kids playing there, and we played football with the kids. They probably never saw a football before, but we had fun playing.

We went to Puerto Rico. We lived in a rental house. There was lizards running around all over the place, and a lady next door was burning something in her backyard, with splashes of gasoline, that made the fire hotter. My father had a box of Snack Pack pudding, and gave it to a family next door. My father said in Spanish it was for the good boys, and girls. We drove around in a yellow VW beatle. When we passed a military base, my father told us to get down in the seat. He was worried they might start shooting at us.

Next we went to Niagara Falls, and Toronto. We went on the "Maiden of the Mist". With black raincoats that give you, because you would get wet. We went to a wax museum in Toronto, and that's all I remember.

Then we went to Hawaii, via L.A. where we went with our cousins the Johnsons, who lived in California. Five of us and five of them. We flew down to Hawaii on QANTAS airlines, and the Johnsons flew on Continental.

At the airport we hired a van with two Hawaiian guys in it. One guy drove the van, and the other guy played Hawaiian songs on guitar. We drove to a couple tourist areas.

The first day in Waikkie beach, at the Sheraton hotel, we went to the beach, but our mother's said the curent was to strong, and wouldn't allow us to go in, so we swam in the hotel pool. The next day we were in the hotel rooms with sunburn. We used jars of Noxzema, to cool our burns, and we had little boxes of cereal for breakfast.

Then we went to Pearl Harbor, and saw the USS Arizona memorial. Christopher was in a cast at the time. He had many childhood diseases. Both of his legs were in a cast with a bar in the middle that kept his legs apart. He accidently dropped his crutches off the balcony, to the balcony below us. My father told me to go down on the elevator, and get the crutches. I went down to the wrong floor, and I actually went down to the lowest floor first, knocked on the door of the room below us, and was met by a Japanese guy. I explained to him what happened, and he went to his balcony while I waited by the door. He gave me the crutch and I said thanks. Meanwhile the tourists from the balcony below us, saw the crutch, and passed it up to us.

Christopher also had a bleeding lung disease. He had to take pregnasone for it, and that's what gave him the chipmunk cheeks.

Back on the trip to Hawaii, we went to a McDonalds, and they were running a special, where if they couldn't get your order ready in less than 3 minutes you get it free. With my father ordering for a family of five, there was no way they could get it done in time. So we got free food.

We went to a mountain, and me and my cousin Peter, were throwing rocks of the cliff. So Christopher decides he was gonna throw rocks too. He threw it and it hit me in the head. Then a guard came up and said we couldn't throw rocks off the cliff because the place was sacred. I think we saw Diamond Head volcano too.

We took many flights to L.A., to see the Johnsons. They lived in Simi Valley, in a modest home. They preferred to go on a lot of vacations.

One trip to L.A. me and Chris were sitting behind this guy in front of us, and his air vent was turned toward us, and was blowing the cold air on us. We didn't like it, so we turned the jet on his bald head and in like 5 minutes he felt the air freezing his head and he turned the air off. It was the funniest thing we ever did together.

Another trip to LA, was on an L-1011. We were in first class in the middle seats, my dad was flying co-pilot. The chairs could rotate around and face backwards, and you could put a table leaf in the middle and seat 4. So we had dinner, the four of us, my mother, brother, sister, and I.

Another trip I was in first class with my brother, and I had an Oakland A's hat on. And Tony Orlando was behind us. I got his autograph on a picture, he printed. And it said "John keep hitting home runs, the A's could use you"!"

We went to Magic Mountain, and Disney Land. We also went to Tijuana, Mexico. You don't need a passport, provided that you don't go south of Tijuana.

Chapter 8
More Middle School

For years I never knew, when you throw a basketball, you were supposed to let it spin backwards, I always thought the ball spun forward, that's why I sucked at it.

Lunch time was fun. We used to spin coins around on the table and they battled against the other coins, knocking them flat. You could keep your coin going by flicking it. As long as it was still spinning you were alive. You could flip the coin off the table and save it, and palm it and throw it back on the table and keep spinning it, as long as it didn't lie flat. Then you were out.

The school had dances on Friday nights. We picked up my friend Brad Ashley. In middle school your hair was important. One night we picked Brad up and he got in the car. And he was mad because the wind blew his hair. He had had it just the way he liked. I laughed.

But at the dance they had a disco ball on the ceiling. And a make out corner, where couple would pair off and sit on the floor and kiss and pet.

The school had two one way halls, but at the bell you could run up the wrong way, and get to class without going all the way around. Me and my friend Tom Ziggy, started to notice girls. One girl we liked had a big nose, but we said "Big nose has big tits." And we liked her. In Spanish class the teacher was fat. She always started each class by saying "escho

18

me" which means listen to me. My name is John, Guillermo in Spanish. And Tom called me "gay-homo". But his name was Timotayo, in Spanish. And I called him Tim-o-gay-o. Touchea. Needless to say we never teased each other like that again.

Chapter 9
7th Grade

In the seventh grade I moved away from my family at the house, to stay at my aunt Fran's house, in Burlington, MA. My cousins, John, Gilbert, and Andrea were close friends, but at the end of the school year, me and John were at each other's throats.

I played organized soccer, and broke my arm making a soccer move on the ball. I had a cast on it and they wouldn't let me play. I was like "why not, you don't use your hands in soccer anyways. I itched it one day, and stuck a pen in there to scratch it, but the cap fell off and got stuck inside. I had to take the cast off prematurely, because the cap hurt my arm.

I had a paper route, but I hated it. The customers never paid on time.

Me and John were in a trivia contest at school, we beat the other team and won a trophy.

Chapter 10
8th Grade

Back at 8th grade in PA., my father and I went to a Philadelphia Fever game..It was a major indoor soccer league game. That was cool. I bought a USA hockey t-shirt.

Then tragedy struck our family. My parents got divorced. One day my mother, brother, and sister, got into my uncle's van and headed to Gloucester, MA. I was supposed to go with them, but I didn't want to leave all my friends. So I ran into the barn, and hid in the hayfort. They left me there. I went to school, and my father showed up in the boys locker room, after gym class. We hugged each other and went to the Quakertown mall, to buy me new clothes, because my mother took all mine with her.

So there we were, the two of us, alone in that big old house. But my father still had to fly for TWA. So we hired a series of house keepers, that would watch me while my father was away on trips. First we had Dee, and her daughter. That didn't work out. Then we had a beautiful model woman, could have easily been in a playboy magazine. She had boots on that go up her leg or she could roll them down below her knees. And she said when she walked in the door, "let's not just hire me because I'm beautiful". But we were like do you want the job or not. So we hired her. And she was cool. She used to give me rides to school, when the bus driver kicked me off the bus for throwing the paper at the bucket. That worked for a while but didn't last too long.

Then there was a nice old lady who watched me. I used to go to my friend Lorne's after school, to play with him. He was actually my brother's friend, but when he moved away he became my friend. He had an inground swimming pool too, with a spa. We swam in there through underwater hoops, where we played a game of chase. You could only tag the player if you were in the same hoop as him.

Lorne had the Mattel Intelevision game. We played it all day long, and watched MTV and played Dungeons and Dragons, with painted pewter miniatures that he had.

I drove my Kawasaki KE 100 to his house, but I always had trouble going without stalling it. One day I was late and my housekeeper came over to get me. She was mad. But it wasn't my fault, I couldn't get the bike to go.

Finally we had Skip. He use to work at JUST BORN. The jelly bean maker that Ronald Reagan used to eat. One day I skipped school, and knew I wasn't going because I didn't take a shower that morning. He must of seen me sneak into the barn, and he left me a chore list to do. I didn't do it. I think.

Then one day my father, and I, and my friend Brad, went to Kansas City, to the amusement park., Worlds of Fun. We pretended Brad was my brother so he could fly for free too, and we flew to Missouri. They had a rollercoaster called the Orient Express, that we read about. It went upside down 4 times. When the park opened for the day, the three of us ran down to the Orient Express, before anybody else and got first in line. Me and my father in front for the first ride, then me and Brad got in front for the second ride. That's all I remember from Worlds of Fun.

But Brad was a good friend. He showed me how to ride my motorcycle. I went to his house one night, we watched the movie Midnight Express. He had two beautiful sisters, Jackie, and Sandy. One day I was in the basement and I looked out the window. To my surprise Sandy was crouched down by the window, doing some gardening. I couldn't help it I had a clear view of her breasts. Lucky me.

Chapter 11
High School

One guy I forgot was Jerry Shore, he was a Karate instructor, and he drove a camaro with an American flag on the roof. He was supposed to pick me up from school. High school. We were the Southern Lehigh Spartans. He was going to drive me home, but I wasn't sure if he would come or not, so I ran to catch the bus home. He would have introduced to me to Marijuana.

At school, the gym teacher saw that I had good hands, and he wanted me on the team. But I didn't want to play, because I was embarrassed by my body. At lunch we ate in the smaller cafeteria. You had to watch because whole hoagies or hamburgers could fly at you. I sat with some kids but then I wasn't cool enough to sit with them any more. And my friend Tom Ziggy said I could sit with him. He was a good friend.

Tom had a 6 wheel Amphibious vehicle. We took it for a ride one day. But the thing couldn't make right turns. To go right you had to take 3 left turns. We drove down the road by his house, and Tom flipped it over on me. It went down an embankment and we couldn't get it out. Tom was thinking we had to get his riding lawn mower to pull it out, but luckily he was able to drive it out. We had to do this against the clock, because his father was coming home soon, and Tom would get in trouble. Then I flipped it over on him, in his field and got revenge.

We were walking through his field behind his house, one day. With bb guns, and he shot me with a bb, in the hip. I returned fire and got him. Then I said 'Let's not shoot each other anymore before someone losses an eye. I had a little bit of weed, and me and Tom, and my friend from elementary school, Dave Butterwisk, had some weed too. We got high.

One day at school somebody flushed a cherry bomb down the toilet, and it exploded. They were offering $1000 reward to anybody who would tell them who did this. This guy they called the wolfman because of his beard. Kids used to say "oh, the wolfman was howling at me today."

Students were wild there. They let a greased pig in the school one year. A year later they let loose 100 white mice. And the year I was there they chained the doors of the stairways with lock and chain. Nobody could go up or down, til they brought in bolt cutters. There was like a ten minute delay in getting to class.

You had to be careful with your books on the stairways, because Steve Appleton would try to punch my books out from under my arm on the stairs, where everybody would just kick them around. You had to carry your books in your right arm or else.

The pot smoking kids (the vocational crowd) were called speds. And they wore sped boots. I wanted some sped boots so I could be cool. I pleaded with my father to buy me some, and he did. I loved my sped boots.

One night I slept over at Tom's house, me and my friend Fred Money. They dared me to go in his sister's room, where she was sleeping. I did. I went into the room and she told me to get out. It's a good thing his father didn't hear me.

I said goodbye to my friend Gary Bolt. At the last day of school. I was moving away to Kentucky with my father. That was it for Southern Lehigh High School.

Chapter 12
Kentucky

My father and I moved to KY, the following year, to Flatwoods, KY, and Russell High School. I was first met there by Tim Meuller, my father's friend's son. I slept over his house one night, and he introduced me to AC/DC's TNT. I liked it.

The first day of school, he introduced me to all his friends. I said hello but I really didn't say much at all. I had the words in my mouth but I didn't utter them. He introduced me to Fran Banner. And I was going to say to her "marry me and you won't have to change your last name." But I didn't say it. After all the introductions were done, everybody headed to class. One guy remained, and wanted me to say something, but I held my peace. 10th grade was very boring for me.

My father and I had to find a house, but there really weren't many homes available. So my father made a smart move and bought a mobile home. It was 70' by 14'. I had to find it in the trailor park after the first day of school. I met a new friend Glen. He lived in a mobile home too, across the street from the trailor park, with his mother.

I found my father, and I loved the trailor. It was 3 bedrooms, bath and a half, living room, and kitchen, with a long counter top, with stools, for eating, and table and chairs.

But dad still had to work for TWA, so we had to find a housekeeper to watch me while he was away.

One girl was very nice, she kept a tidy house, her name was Corrine. But her boyfriend, Bob Stork, (the biggest bad ass around) was jealous because he thought we were having sex. But we convinced him we were not. And we became friends. He told me that anybody who wanted to mess with me was gonna have to mess with him. It was great to have a bodyguard.

At school, the Russell Red Devils, in 10th grade, we were friends, Kevin Hart, Rick Stone, and Larry Valerio. One day in science class Valerio scratched my hand with his fingernails. So I took a pencil and broke the tip off, leaving a jagged pencil point, and I stabbed it into Valerio's hand. He yelled and I ran down the isle of desks. The teacher said "John!" I sat down and life went on.

We were talking about music, and I told Rick, Genesis had a good album to buy. It had many hit songs. One day after class we were walking out the door, and Valerio goes "come on shadow"! He called me "shadow", somehow I disasoutiated myself from the group. I let them walk on, and I went on by myself. Some how my right brain lost a part of socializing. I didn't follow them anymore, I went my own path.

Chapter 13
11th Grade

11th grade was great. My father bought me my first car. A black Chevy II Nova. And 350 v8, and 411 gears of possy traction. We had to go to some airport in Ohio to pick it up. But we drove it home from there. And we were driving, and my father said "step on the gas" so I floored it and it took off like a rocket ship. That 4 barrel carb kicked in. Later on I put Goodyear Eagle tires on it and Crager wheels.

But before I drive my nova, I had to get my license. I went to the Greenup county courthouse, and get tested. My aunt Kathryn lent me her car to take the test in. A big Chevy Capris. The first test I took, the police officer said "back it up". So I swung my arm over the seat to look behind me, and I accidently knocked his hat off his head. Needless to say, I didn't pass the test that day.

The next day I took the test again and passed it. I also brought my motorcycle, the Kawasaki, to get tested. It was a lady's first day on the job, and she didn't know anything about motorcycles. The test was in a small parking lot. You had to go through 3 gears and turn around, and come back. I passed the test easily. Two other guys were getting their tests done on big bikes. I didn't stay to watch them. So I got my license and my first car.

Chapter 14
The Partying Days

Me and my friend Glen, we joined together with two friends, Steve Gobert, and Eric Flounder, who lived in nice houses, within walking distance to my trailor. Every night when my father was away on trips, we partied. When the time came it was your job to get everybody high for the week. We took turns buying a bag of pot, and you got everybody high for the week.

The first time I tried Marijuana, I didn't get off. I didn't see what the big deal was. But my friends told me I was doing it wrong. It took me three separate times to get off. I didn't know you had to hold the smoke in your lungs, until you had to breathe again. One day we were in the woods, and I smoked a joint, and I finally got high. I laughed and I laughed.

At the trailor me and Rick got high and we used to play Acey Duecy backgammon. We would get stoned and play Risk. The trailor had a built in 8 track player in the wall, with 4 speakers on the ceiling. 2 speakers in the living room, and 2 speakers in my room. My father took the bedroom with the 1/2 bath. We played REO Speedwagon's "High Infidelity" 8 track over and over. We just let it run.

One night we had a party, with the 4 of us, and some burnout friends, the ones who got me high the first time. We were playing Boston's Don't Look Back, and we had 3 radios going, in the living room. Somehow the connections of the 3 radios, was broadcasting over the citizens band radio. We heard them through the speakers "we'll get these kids" "there playing that rock music somewhere in Flatwoods" we quickly shut two radios off, and they never found us.

But we didn't always party at the trailor, we would take my Nova out for joy rides. We would go over the bridge to Centerville, Ohio, where the drinking age for beer was 19. There was one store that has a drive through, and they sold to minors. We used to get a case of Little Kings. But Steve, and Rick liked Canadian beer too. So we always used to get Labbatt's Ale for Rick, and Moosehead beer for Steve.

Sometimes we would go to West Virginia, where the drinking age was 18, to buy our hard stuff. We bought gallon bottles of Jack Daniels, Jim Beam, and Old Mr. Boston 100 proof vodka. Then we would get Lawrence fifth of screwdriver, and drink it down to a point on the lable, and drink the rest of it before school the next day.

I stayed at Glen's mother's trailor sometimes too. One night we were partying with screwdrivers and pot. I was supposed to go to Glen's house for the night. I was the last one in the trailor after everybody went home. And I was drinking screwdrivers, and Glen's mother kept calling me to come home, and she called me like 4 times. And I said "yes I'll be right over." I was drunk of my ass. And I finally went to Glen's house. On the porch of my trailor, I fell off and landed in a mud pile passed out. My neighbor came home and saw me lying there. He picked me up and helped me across the street to Glen's house.

I walked in the door and fell on my face. Glen's mother, Sally, said John you are drunk", and I said "yes", and she said "get your ass back to bed". I laid down in Glen's bed and through the night, the alcohol seeped through my pore, and the bed became soaked. The next morning I went to school, still drunk from the night before. I was in the hallway at school, bouncing off lockers.

One day we drove to a wooded area. We had a case of Little Kings, and we got stoned with a bong. We went into the woods and tripped out. It was warm the day before, but the next day it was cold, and we found a lizard petrified. He was froze because he got caught in the cold. We put him in the bong, and smoked through it. He came to life and tried to get out but he couldn't. My friend Harry Red spun the bong around and around but

I stopped him and I brought the lizard home and had him as a pet for a couple years, and I named him Godzilla.

My friend Dave Kazoo had a little chevy 4 door sedan, with an excellent stereo system in it. We used to trade vehicles, he would drive my motorcycle, while I drove his car around. We would get stoned and just drive around listening to music. One night I did a half a quallude with Dave. He dropped me off somewhere in my trailor park, and that's the last thing I remember from that night.

Back at the trailor, we partied hard. We always used to smoke a bong with ice in it. We used a tiny little one hit bowl, and passed it around. Each of our four got a little one hit bowl, that way we didn't waste any smoke, and we didn't waste any pot.

One night it was me, Steve, Rick, and our friend Baron. Me and Baron sat at the counter, while Steve, and Rick, were seated on the side. We were stoned. Then I said to Baron, "Baron!" I called his name and I rolled around on the floor, laughing hysterically, for like 10 minutes. Then I regained my composure, and I sat down next to Baron again. And I said "Baron!" again and I rolled on the floor for another 10 minutes laughing. Everybody laughed.

Another night, me, Baron, Steve, and Rick. Went to Portsmouth, Ohio. I drove my father's Buick Riviera. Baron was going to buy a pound of weed. We got to the pizza joint, in Portsmouth. The guys there gave us some weed to smoke, and it was excellent pot. We thought we were buying a pound of this weed, but they tricked us and sold us a pound of shake. We were serious pot heads, and somehow we got fooled.

So Baron played the same trick right back to a kid in our neighborhood, Spaz. We got him high, with some good pot, then sold him the pound of shake. Baron got his money back and Spaz got burned.

One night me, Steve, Glen, and Rick were driving in the Buick Riviera. We were in Ashland, KY, and we drove along some guy in a Datsun B 210. He held up a little bottle of Jack Daniels. Then Steve held up our gallon bottle of Jack Daniels. I put the hammer down, and we left him in the dust. We all laughed.

One day me and Glen, and a bunch of my burnout friends who got me high the first time, took a ride to Ashland to see an abandoned haunted house. There was about 8 of us squeezed into the Buick. We got to the house and explored around. One room had a 1000 letters scattered on the floor. We checked it out then drove home.

Back at the trailor, we used to get high and listen to Pink Floyd. One song was "one of these days". We played it over and over again. Finally we figured it out that they were saying "one of these days I'm going to cut you into little pieces". Pink Floyd was our favorite trip music. In 1979 when Pink Floyd's The Wall came out, I used to know every lyric to every song on the whole double album.

One night we had a gallon of Jim Beam, and me, Steve, and Rick got drunk in Glen's barn. Me and Rick wrestled all night.

We tripped on acid, and threw rocks, and sticks at each other with the intent to maim. I ate 4 acid drops, not at one time, yellow barrel, purple microdot, orange sunshine, and strawberry mesc. Glen told me that the reason you trip is because your losing so many brain cells at once that the brain freaks out. I recommend that you never do acid.

Chapter 15

Concerts

My first concert was Triumph, in Huntington, WV. I was standing there, in the concert, when I saw my burnout friend. I remember they had a big lighted up sign that said TRIUMPH.

Next me and Glen saw Ozzy Osbourne, in Charleston, WV. My father dropped us off and we went inside. It was a pretty good show. Ozzy had the keyboardist in a tower to the left of the stage. Then he had a giant hand come out with a drum set on it. People were smoking pot, and Glen wanted to try it, but I didn't.

Next I saw Aerosmith, with me, Glen, Tim Meuller, and Dan O'Conner. It was the first ever concert for MTV. The stage floor was white, while a fenced in area held the camera on a boom. People were packed into the area in front of the walled camera, so many in fact that the space between the stage and the camera started to knock down the wall that kept the audience out of the camera area. I don't know why I went to see Aerosmith, I hate them.

Then I saw Lover Boy with Harry Red, in Charleston, WV. That was so so.

Then I saw Iron Madien, and Judas Priest. Iron Maiden had Eddie the big monster guy on stage, who all he did was bob his head up and down. Iron Maiden sucked. Judas Priest blew them away. They were playing music from their album 'screaming for vengeance. At the end they had a Harley, Rob Halford rode out on stage. They held the microphone to the exhaust and wailed it. While Rob was singing, he singled me out in the crowd and started to sing right to me, as if we were the only ones in the concert. It was pretty neat.

Lastly I saw Ozzy again, his "speak of the devil" album. He had no hair.

Chapter 16
Voc School

Voc school saved me from the daily grind of school. I took carpentry class. I didn't know jack about carpentry, but after that first year we built a house. At break we would climb into the dormers of the house we built, and get high. The instructors name was Wilbur Ison. One day Steve stole a case of mountain dew from the coke truck. We all had free mountain dew though it was warm. I used to sit on the belt sander on the floor and grab the trigger with my hand and balanced myself on the sander, then I squeezed the trigger and shot across the floor. We had a contest to see who could carry the most 2x4"s. Barry Glove carried 14 at one time, the record. On rainy days I used to bring my motorcycle into the shop.

There was a skills competition with all the area schools. Dave Kazoo entered the house competition and won. You had to build a little house, with a room about 4 feet big, with little walls, and little dormers. I entered the job interview contest, but didn't win.

Waiting for voc school was lunch for 11th grade I didn't eat in the cafeteria. I hung out with the burnouts, they used to call them hoods in the smoking area, though I didn't smoke. Some of the girls saw me through the window, and I could tell they were scared I was going down the wrong path. But I knew what I was doing. God would enter my path one day.

Chapter 17

12th Grade

In 12th grade me and Tim had psychology class with Mr. Wallenfelz. He was the original Great Karnak. He knows the answer before you read the question. One of his students went on to become a writer for Johnny Carson, and he told him about the Great Karnak (Mr. Wallenfelz), and Johnny incorporated it into his show. I was an honor student in psychology. We had to draw a picture of a nightmare. I copied a cover of a game I had, a dragon breathing fire on a warrior holding his shield to block the flames, then I put a hand in space above the dragon holding a chain around the dragon's neck. I didn't come in the top 3, but I got honorable mention. We were lucky to have him for a teacher, because he retired a few years later. He used to have a fascination with boogers. There was all kinds of boogers, loose boogers, vibrating boogers, and he had a whole collection of windup toys. Snoopy, Woodstock, a car that sped across the floor, flipped over on its back, and drove back the opposite way. He would wind up like 10 of these toys at once and have them dance around on his desk.

Twelfth grade voc saw Steve and Rick gone. I never saw them again, except Steve one last time with my brother. I said I had a headache, and he said "I have some weed that will fix that.!" We got high for the last time.

Twelfth grade lunch something was wrong with me. I used to go to the boys bathroom and sit on the last stall toilet, pretending to go to the

35

bathroom. One day I did this and the principal came in and checked the stalls, but stopped short at the stall next to me, and didn't see me. He walked away and I was about to say "WAIT", but I didn't he left the bathroom, and I left the bathroom a little while later.

I couldn't socialize with people. But I got over it with a little help from my friend Peter Clyde. Peter was my friend at 12th grade voc school. I hung out with him at lunch waiting for voc school to start. We always hung out with the carpentry class kids, at lunch, and we talked to girls. The one I wanted already had a boyfriend, but I was too stupid to say the heck with her, and go with her friend. Who was also very nice, and built. I wish Peter would have told me to go with her.

One day me, and Peter, and another kid, and Barry Glove, and another ROTC guy, we went swimming at Greenbow lake. While we were driving there Peter said I was his best friend. I felt honored that I was somebody's best friend. And I said he was my best friend. We had fun building a house that year.

Some days my friend Ralph, and I would drive to the taco bell in Ashland for lunch. We sneaked past the principal and drove his car or mine to the taco bell.

Peter and I were good friends. We never smoked pot. We used to walk in the woods by his house. Then we used to make 1lb. hamburgers, and we used to eat raw eggs from the shell, becuase we believed it was a food for better sex, with chicks. Peter used to drive his family car, a dodge. We were at a light one day, and the old ladies in the car next to us got ahead of us, and Peter exclaimed 'I let the old lady get the jump on me.

It was funny in 12th grade we moved the trailor to my aunt Kathryn's farmhouse. We parked it on the side of the road. And my father's new wife, Dawn, who he married the year before, and her 3 daughters moved in. My father built an addition off the backdoor. It was a bedroom, an area for his desk, and a living room. We had satellite tv, and there was a sliding glass door with 3 panes of glass. There was also a space that we put under the trailer. There was 3 different doors you had to open in different ways to get the freezer.

One day my step sister was taking a shower, and I deployed a trick I read about in a skin mag. I held a mirror under the door to the bathroom, which didn't go all the way to the floor. And she must have seen the mirror, and yelled. I quickly moved to the couch and started to pet the cat. She stood the door and was fuming, but I kept petting the cat like there is nothing wrong, and I refused to look at her. Later I felt bad about it and there was a small pond behind the trailor, and I walked out on the thin ice. And I said to myself, if I fall through the ice that would be my punishment. I didn't fall through. They made me stay in my room.

My father gave me his Datsun 240z rally car. It was red, with a black hood, and black head light panels. It also had a rollbar in the back. After school we would sit in the parking lot racing our engines. The 240 was overreving Bobby Love's VW Beatle. I used to go everyday down Rt. 7, to the highway Rt. 23, to school. I learned every straightaway, every curve, every bridge. One day my father and I were driving home on Rt. 7. I was in the 240 z car, and my father was driving a 1963 Austin Healy. I passed him on a long straightaway. And I didn't stop racing, I beat him home by five minutes. But it was like Micheal Andretti passing Mario Andretti. For the first time.

One day in the z car, me and Peter drove around. We checked out the Twilight zone, a video arcade store. And we lucked out because the radio was playing the Twilight Zone, by Golden Earing at the same time. We parked out front and jammed it. We thought it was pretty cool.

Another day in the Nova, I was coming home from school down Rt. 7, and the car overheated because there was no coolent in it. I raced it home at top speed trying to get home, but the engine blew up, when I almost made it. We put in a new engine but it wasn't very good, it always ran rough.

Chapter 18

Girls in Kentucky

I lost my virginity to Veronica Lark. We did it in my bedroom one night. She wanted to come over every night and have sex. But I didn't want that. I wasn't a Christian but I knew it was wrong.

I went out with Lisa. She was in my Spanish class. I used to sit beside her. We went to the movies one day, and saw a stupid movie. After it was over we made out. A week later we broke up. And at lunch a group of girls told me she still wanted to go out with me. But stupid me, I thought I would look cool if I said no to her. So I lost my girl friend.

I dated a girl in one of my classes, Stephanie East. We both had mesh shirts on, and I noticed she filled her shirt out quite nicely with big breasts. I used to go out with her alot to different spots to have sex. We were making love on the hood of my car one night, in a ball park drive area, when suddenly a car came. We both tried to grab our clothes and hide in the car.

I had Stephanie over at the trailor our first night together. We had sex. Then she says "did we just have sex, or did we make love?" I knew we just had sex but I was smart and figured if I want to do this again. I said "make love." I made love to Stephanie one night in Brad's barn, in the hay loft.

We went to a small party at her friend's house, and we got high. I was going to ask her to take her shirt off, but I didn't.

I slept at her grandmother's house one night. And that was the end of seeing Stephanie.

One day I was alone in the trailor, and the phone rang. I answered and this girl on the other line wanted me to masturbate over the phone. She wanted to hear me unzip. So I held the phone down and unzipped but that was all I did. Then she wanted me to pick her up at the Super Quik. About five minutes later the phone rings again and this guy says to me "John, I know who you are. I know where you live. Don't go to the Super Quik, and get my sister'. So I said "ok". And asked why did she call me. He said "she's young". The information was valuable.

Then Suzy Sierra came over to my house one day. She wanted to get high and have sex. We got high and laid on the bed. Then she wanted me to take my shirt off, but I was too embarrassed by my nipples. So we didn't go any farther.

Another time a girl came over to my door, and she wanted to have sex, but I was to stupid to let her in.

Lastly I met Charlene Bread. She knew about Gloucester, we went out on one date, to her friends house, and made out on the floor. Beside the couch. In 11th grade, she got pregnant, not by me. And her parents made her go to Canada, to escape embarrassment. She came back for 12th grade, but I was too stupid to pursue her.

Chapter 19

The Class Trip and Graduation

The senior class trip was to New York, and Washington, D.C. I didn't go. I stood there and watched as the two buses filled with my graduating class drove away. I told them the excuse I had been there before. Again the anti-socializing. We had the prom, I didn't go.

Then we had graduation practise. Everyone was seated in the gym. I was late, driving my father's Austin Healy. I walked in and said something funny. Everybody laughed. I think I said I want to go one more year. I was going to say something else, that would have made a laugh riot, but I held my tongue.

Graduation night I was late for the ceremony. I drove my Nova to the school, and got stopped by the police for speeding. I had my gown on and I told him I was late for graduation. He let me go and, and I got to graduation, and dad took a picture of me standing between my mother, and mother in law, Dawn. My mother said I was a rose between two thorns.

They told us not to throw our hats after the closing part of the ceremony. I wanted all of us to do it. But in the end some did, but I didn't. After the graduation we went to Tim Mueller house for the class party. I wasn't going to miss this. I went with Peter, who was only a junior, but I snuck him in. This one girl was there that I dated, Devonna Shorter. She was passed out on the bed, next to some guy, passed out. I squeezed her boob. Tim had a keg of beer there, I only had one cup. But all of a sudden Laura from psychology class was there in the kitchen. And we went like magnets, kissing each other. Everybody in the kitchen was shocked. I wanted to take her home, but she left without me. And that was it for life in Kentucky.

Chapter 20
A Return to Elementary School Days

We put on a dance recital at elementary school. I was in a lineup of four boys, we had top hats, and canes. We were supposed to do a dance routine. I would have done the recital, but my father took us to Alabama, to see my grandmother. Alabama is the most boring place in the world. There is nothing to do there. So that's another key moment in life in my development that I missed.

Then I played midget football. I was on the 85lb. b team. We were good, we won our division. I played fullback and safety. Our first game was a scrimmage match against Quakertown. I caught a touchdown pass. Then on the extra point attempted I had the ball and made it to the goal line. I should have pushed the ball across the line, but I didn't do it. We tied the game at 6-6. On their extra point attempt I made a key tackle that stopped them from scoring their extra point.

After the season was over, about 8 of us the best players on the team went on to play for the 85lb. A team. But then we had to go to Alabama again to see my grandmother. My parents pulled me out of the practise squad, and I didn't get to play with them. Once again I missed a major event in my life.

One day after football practise, we went to the Fright Castle. A medium sized house used by the jaycees to host a spook house. About 3 of us went, still in our football uniforms. The signs said "some scenes are gory, some scenes are bloody. People with heart problems shouldn't go in." We went in and immediately I was scared. There were actors in all the scenes. They had people coming over the top of the wall, and grabbing you. Then they had holes in the wall by your feet., and they would grab your ankles. We had our cleats on and when they did that we stepped on their hands, and you could hear them say "ow" behind the wall.

One scene was Frankenstein. I don't know what it is about Frankenstein but he scares the hell out of me. He was on a table, and the scientist leaned his table up, and Frankenstein came off. He headed right towards me. I shrunk down in a corner of the room, and I did not want to go on. But my friend Eric Money said "its all right John, its just make belief." So I got over it. But the wolfman was right around the corner. He was in a steel cage, and he had a fat bat, wiffle ball bat. He was banging it against the bars, and he scared me too. Finally we got out of Fright Castle. What a relief.

Chapter 21

Back to Kentucky for A Minute

Me and Glen, and Steve, and Rick had a hut in the woods, behind Glen's trailor. Me and Spaz were in their one morning, before school getting high, and Spaz lit the wall on fire. He put it out but later we learned that the fire had rekindled. Glen's mother had to call the fire dept. to put it out. The fire burned the hut completely. I was mad because I had 2 240 z car seats in there.

Glen's grandmother had a field by her house. And Glen, and Rick, and I used to drive Glen's grandmother's car through the field of tall grass. That was fun.

One day we stumbled over a pair of 22's hand guns, from Spaz. Me, and Steve, and Rick, went to my aunt Kathryn's house in Greenup County to shoot them. Then we decided to turn the guns over to the police, saying we found them. My friend who was in the army, cleaned them. Then we called the police over to my trailor and invited them in, two cops. They put their fingers all over the cleaned guns, and took them into custody. We got rid of the guns, and laughed because they put their finger prints all over the 22's.

Another day in school, I was in class, and this combination burp, hiccup from my lungs produced a little puff of smoke. It smelled like weed so bad, I thought the whole class could smell it. I had been carrying around this much weed in my system, just a little puff of smoke came out.

I let my friend Dave Kazoo, borrow my cassette player with head phones, and he tripped out on Pink Floyd.

One day my father wanted to have done a cosmetic surgery on me. I had dumbo ears, and we had a surgeon cut away the cartilage, and pin my ears back. I had to wear a bandage around my head for a day. After surgery Glen's mother came in to see me in the hospital. I saw her and said "hello Mrs. Salyers"! Then I passed out from the anesthesia.

But the stupid jackass surgeon, left one stitch in my right ear. Years later a dentist took hemostats and pulled it out. After surgery I could hear sounds 10x better. But this may have been the cause of hearing voices later in life, I don't know.

Back at the trailer when we were living on aunt Kathryn's land in Greenup county, I learned a trick I read in Playboy magazine. That you could hold a mirror, under the door, and see inside. One day my stepsister was taking a shower, and I held the mirror under the door, and saw her naked. She caught me because she saw the mirror. I immediately sat on the couch. She came out and was standing behind me probably fuming, I don't know, because I didn't look at her, I just petted the cat, like there was nothing wrong.

When my father found out he punished me to my room, and I couldn't come out. I didn't care because I was watching the Olympics on tv.

But I felt so bad for what I did that I walked out on the thin ice of a small pond we had behind the trailer. I figured if I fell through the ice that would be my punishment. I walked out but the ice held, and I didn't fall through. Nobody knows that I did this, just me and God, and now you.

Now that was the end of Kentucky for now.

Chapter 22

Massachusetts

In the summer of 1983, I worked as a carpenter in Gloucester. We were building a garage onto the home of the Ekborg's. We also built the 2nd floor of Charlies Place restaurant. It was a good summer job. I remember I went to a graduation party in E. Gloucester. I was drinking beer, but switched to screwdrivers. I got real drunk, and went behind the house to throw up. I stood there clutching the fence and trying to stay upright. People came and saw me hanging on. I was wasted. Then we went to a large room with no furniture upstairs. We sat in a square around the four corners of the room, and got high. The vodka and the weed was too much for me. I just sat there on the floor totally gone, and pointing my finger at whoever was staring at me. That night might have been a cause for mental illness later in life. I don't know.

The summer of 1984 I moved to MA. for good. Being with mom, Chris, and Cathy at 9 White's Mtn. Rd. My uncle Jack built the house, we called it the house that Jack built. It had a great beam down the center of the house. Jack walked across it as we all stood by and watched him. There was 3 bedrooms, another room, laundry room, kitchen, and living room.

Me and all the kids from the neighborhood used to party there. Central to the house was the deck. Kids were throwing beer bottles in to the woods across the driveway. I told them to stop.

My mother had a boyfriend, Will Heart. He used to sit around and watch porno videos. So one day he didn't want my mother to throw him out, so he purposely jumped out the sliding glass door next to the porch and broke his leg. I guess he figured if he was banged up my mother wouldn't throw him out. He had his leg in a cast on one day he was on the porch smoking a cigarette. I didn't like him, and I wanted to fight him. So I went up to him, and wasn't go to say anything at all, but when I got up to him I said "defend yourself". I took a couple of swings at him, then I got him in a side head lock. I tried to ram his head into the doorway. He said "if you let me go, I won't tell you mother." I didn't care if he told my mother so I rammed his head into the door. The fight broke up and he told my mother, but nothing became of it. She broke up with him shortly thereafter.

Chapter 23
Jobs

In the summer of 1984, I worked for the moonies, as a dishwasher. I quickly left that bullshit job, for food prep. I used to dip the shrimp, clams, and scallops in the batter to fry them. Then I got promoted to fry cook. I loved it, I worked the fryolater and grill. I used to steal a clam or two off orders and eat them.

My friend Bobby Monroe used to work the lunch shift, and I worked the dinner shift. He would always pick me up after work. Part of the job was going to the lobster company at the corner of the parking lot, and get lobsters for the restaurant.

There was Japanese girls there and they made delicious rice balls. I invited two of them to my house after work one day. My mother thought I was going to become a moonie. There was also a couple of Japanese guys there too. They took notes on how to make a hamburger. I used to go into the cooler and suck all the air out of the whipped cream bottle to get high. The manager went in their and saw the bottles, he thought they were delivered that way.

Sometimes I would eat the dinner that the headchef Paul, made for all the moonies. The food had saltpeter in it, to keep the sexual desires of the moonies in check. They all slept in cubicles under the restaurant. The restaurant's name was called the Lobster Pond Restaurant. They did pretty good business with all the tourists. Locals would drive by and yell "moonies suck"!

I was an excellent fry cook, and had to clean the fryolators at night before we could go home. I had 3 girlfriends there, all waitresses. One girlfriend on a date was Nancy Moore. I went on a date with her in her neighborhood in Annisquam village. We were walking and talking, and suddenly I realized that I was talking to her, and she stopped walking, and I kept walking and talking, for about 20-25 yards, when I realized she wasn't beside me anymore. I had to walk back in embarrassment.

Then I went out with Rose. And Bobby went out with Clair. We had a deal to see who could have sex with these two girls. Bobby had sex with Clair, and I had sex with Rose. I used to sleep at her house, then she would sleep at my house, when I was living with my Uncle Dave's house. Bobby came into my rom one morning, and started gabbing about all the things we were going to do that day. He didn't see Rose there.

We did cocaine one night at my mother's other house on Brooks Rd. I let Rose drive my Nova up White's Mtn. Rd. She purposely hit every pot hole. I pushed her when we got out. I thought I would never hit a woman, I didn't hit her, but I pushed her. One night I went to her house, I didn't want to have sex, I just wanted to sleep there. She said no, and I went home. That was the end of Rose.

One night the manager took all the employees to see Purple Rain with Prince. Then we went to Crane's beach and he gave money to the person who could jump the farthest distance in the sand, I won easily. Then we went to a restaurant in Newburyport, and we had full carafes of margaraita. I got drunk and rode back with Sammy Cinammon, and my friend Paul Temple's mother. He smoked a joint, and I was wasted. I don't know how I got home that night.

The moonies used to have a fleet of tuna boats. That's what they did every morning, was go out on these boats, called One Hope, and a number. Like One Hope 22, and One Hope 30, etc. Me, and Bobby went tuna fishing with the moonies one day. I got sick, and had to lie down in the bow of the boat for 8 hours. They had a fleet of like 20 boats, and went tuna fishing everyday. That was the end of the moonies.

My next job was building a house on Causeway St. It was a big $250,000 house, and I was getting $ 4.00/hr. I complained and the foreman said he would give me a raise on the next house. I quit after the first one. I always start a project and never get to the next level. I always quit. My friend/cousin Stoney, worked with us, a couple days, on the roof when we needed an extra hand. The house was beautiful, blue.

In 1986 I worked at the paint factory for $6.10/hr. What a great job. I am proud today that I can say I worked at Gloucester's iconic paint factory. What a trip inside and out. When you first walk through the main door, there is a breakroom, with a picnic table covered with paint splashes. A coffee maker, and a cabinet. To the left side is a bathroom, with a shower for emergencies. As you walk past the two rooms, you come to an area where there is all 55 gallon barrels full of chemicals. Then you make a right and head up a ramp to the main floor. On the left is an area for more 55 gallon barrels, and what they call Opies's jail, where they stored boxes of the k-l line of bottom paints for boats.

On the main floor is where they made the paints. Top and bottom paints. In the next area is the filling station, and label area, where you put labels on cans one at a time both gallons, and quarts.

At the filling station was a huge chain lift to lift 100 gallon tubs of paint on a slanted platform. Then you let the paint flow to a smaller little tub where you fill the cans one at a time. Then while the filler is filling a can, slowly, you would press the lid on a can with a lever on the floor you pressed with your foot. Then the lid was pressed onto the can and sealed. The full can of paint was then put into a cardboard box, 4 gallons to a box, and 6 quarts to a box. The boxes were then dollied off to the storage area in the next room.

I used to love putting the labels on cans, because it was fun. I made forts of bags of labeled cans, and the rock music playing loudly.

Then the foreman, Pete Dumas, must have thought that I was having too much fun labeling, that he put me on packing. Each Monday you would get your position for the week, and one month he had me packing for a month straight. That sucked. I complained to the guys, and felt their sympathy.

One thing that I did that was a lot of fun was making the batch of kl concentrate, a main ingredient of the kl line of paints. It was made up of gallons of copper oleate, copper naphenate, copper carbonate, a powder, mineral spirits, which we jokingly called evil spirits, and rosin, a crystal that you ground up into powder. Pouring it into a 100 gallon tub with a propeller on a shaft to mix it.

One day my friend Jim Spiro, was making a batch of kl concentrate, and he put too much chemicals in it, and it boiled over. Just a huge mess of green chemicals all over the floor. The mixture seeped through the cracks on the floor boards, and poured to the next floor, like green spaghetti strings from the top floor, to the 2nd floor, to the 1st floor, to the basement. What a disaster! Amazingly he didn't get a fired.

Another time we were pushing a 100 gallon tub across the floor, and it was so heavy it crashed through the floor. Paint sloshed over the side of the tub. They had to get a 2 ton floor jack to lift it out of the hole the tub created. They had kitty litter for just this type of calamity, and they sprinkled some around the paint to sop it up.

They had a night shift of just 3 guys, from 4-12am, a filler, a packer, and a paint maker. We had to do inventory one night, and had to measure with a yard stick all the barrels of chemicals, and all the paint in stock. That was fun.

Once I took it upon myself to sweep the entire floor of the rosin room. I swept all the chemical powders in to their respective cubby holes. And the foreman saw it and was well pleased.

Then I ran the chain of the elevator, through the winch and accidently ran it through, and the chain feel to the bottom of the elevator shaft. So I went to the basement, got on top of the elevator roof, and slung the chain over my shoulder. I then climbed up the shaft to the top floor, and reconnected the chain back through the winch, and secured it. I got it done in the nick of time, because the foreman came upstairs to see me, as was his custom.

In the parking lot I used to ride my motorcycle over the rock, against the side of the parking area. I had a Yamaha DT 175 bored out to a 185 Enduro, which I got around on.

But the paint factory was sold in the summer of 1986, and moved the paint business to Rule Industries at the Cape Ann Industrial Park.

I worked for Jones Brothers Insulation Company, I only lasted about two weeks, but I was fired for poor production. I had to turn in my stapler and hammer. One of the things I remember about that job, was that everybody parked their trucks in the back parking lot of a business, and they would all set stoned. I didn't participate, I just stayed in the truck til they were done smoking.

We had to unload the trucks when they came in with more rolls of insulation. I had to work the truck, pushing the bundles of insulation to the guys who would then stack the bundles in the sheds.

It was a so-so job. Every guy showed me how he hangs insulation. One guy said do it this way and another guy said do it this way. So I never developed my own style for hanging insulation.

Then I worked at Manchester Gulf Station, pumping gas. That was a fun job. The best part was at night after closing time, you had to balance the books, how much gas was pumped and how much money was taken in.

One day these guys from Indiana were there, and I asked them who won the Indy 500 this year?, and they didn't know. I said that's a disgrace, two guys from Indiana don't even know who won the Indy 500. They were embarrassed. I have been to the Indy 500 twice. One year there were 3 Mexican cars, and my father and I sat on the back straightaway, and there was a yellow caution, and Mario Andretti got in front of the pack, and got a huge lead. He was coming down the back straightaway, and my father stands up and says "here comes Mario"! Everybody was like "oh Mario"! Then we saw Danny Ongais smash his black 25 racer into the wall at turn 3. The car burst into flames.

Another day a guy with a cccp jacket was there in a van full of mentally ill people. I was looking at him through the window. My prerogative right? So he comes in and says "why are you staring at us?" "Jesus Christ man these people are mentally ill" and I was about to say "and he's the only one who can help them", but I said nothing. Noticing his Russian jacket I was about to say "why don't you go live in Russia? But again I said nothing, I let him drive away. But to my point, this is a gas station, anything outside these windows gets looked at.

Then I worked for the Yankee Fleet, a whole fleet of whale watch boats, and day trips for deep sea fishing. I had to clean the toilets, and pick up cigarette butts, in the waiting area, and collecting and sorting all the cans for redemption. Another part of the job was driving my Nissan pickup truck to Danvers to the B.J's whole sale store and get beer, soda, and candy, for sale on the boats. I built a staging area out of 2x4's in the dumpster area to collect the cans in separate bins. Then I would take the cans to the liquor store, a stones throw away, for returning, and bring the money back to the boss, Tom. That job lasted about two months.

Another job was as a security guard for Allied Security. I had to work the overnight shift 11-7 at Gloucester Engineering at Blackburn Industrial park. I made my rounds 3x/night. One night the sprinkler system went off and all the sprinklers were emitting water. I called the foreman up, who showed up about and hour later, who thought it was no big deal.

Then I worked guarding Sieman's in Danvers. I made the rounds about 3x/night. I then worked guarding a truck yard every night shift. I was in the trailor til it got too dark to see. Then I moved to my Nissan pickup truck, the rest of the night. One guy always came around to the yard to fill all the trucks with gas. Him and I used to talk while he was pumping the trucks. Then I had to guard Gloucester Engineering Sargent St. I made my rounds about 3x/night. I had a little 4 inch tv to watch. I would walk around and always talk to one guy Sam. One week the guys were on strike, we had to double the guards, so two of us worked the same shift. We were in solidarity with the workers, who picketed outside the cafeteria windows. I was going to North Shore Community College at the time and I was doing my math homework. The other guard who was gay, because he wanted to see if I had hair on my legs, said, "home work too important, I'll make the rounds."

I always used to go home at 6:30 am instead of 7 am, not knowing I was supposed to be relieved. I don't think I ever got a paycheck from Allied Security for the 3 months I worked for them.

Then I used to work at Hogan/Berry Mental Retardation Center. I got my house's laundry at the start of shift. Then you put all the clothes away. One guy named Stephen used to sit naked on the floor, just pulling his willy. One guy used to pull your hair when you got next to him. One night God prepared me for what I was about to go through. I was in the kitchen, and when I left a retard named Rocky was covered head to toe in feces. He had it all over him. I put on my rubber gloves and walked him to the bathroom. I had to put him in the shower and wash all the crap off. What a gross thing that was.

Another night there was a loud thud, I heard it but I didn't check it out. And the charge nurse came in and investigated the noise. It seems that one of the retards (for lack of a better name) knocked a chair over. The charge nurse wrote me up.

They soon fired me for not doing a good enough job. I sat down with the guy who fired me, and I got him to agree on giving me all my vacation pay, and sick pay to add to my final paycheck. I got out of there with like $.300.

Then I worked with these guys who were doing fundraisers for police and fire charities. We would go into a given town, and the first thing they would do is solicit hotels to put an ad in the program book in exchange for free hotel rooms then they would sit in little work stations and make cold calls to all the businesses and residences to donate money in exchange for for name listing in the program book. The donor would get tickets to an event for donating, usually a police vs. new England Ice Sharks hockey game, or a wrestling match, or even a Beatles cover group.

I used to drive my Nissan pickup truck to all the residences, and business and pick up checks in envelopes taped to the door, and leave them tickets to the show.

I made half decent money there but I had to buy all my gas myself. Wanted to make the guys give me $3 apiece for gas but it didn't happen.

It was kind of a fun job. I had my map of the town I was in and drove all around picking up checks.

All the guys smoked pot. They'd start the day stoned, and drink beer at night.

One hotel had a pool, and me and another guy raced to see who could swim a lap the fastest. A girl who was working with us (Shannon), who was well endowed, was getting out of the pool. And she was climbing the ladder up, I jumped at the opportunity to see her in that bikini top, that I went to the ladder and offered my hand to help her up, as an excuse to see that bustline. But she said she didn't need help, and got out of the pool herself.

One night she stayed with me and another kid Dave in our room. We had to bring in a cot for the extra person, and it was at the foot of the bed. I moved it to be between the two beds in the middle. A guy came in who was the boss' brother and sees it and says "why do you have the bed in the middle?, 'are you gay?' I could have cleared the air right there by saying "That's so Shannon can watch tv if she wants to." But I said nothing, letting him go thinking bad about me. But when Shannon came into the room for the night, I was going to ask her if she wanted to take a shower with me. But I didn't get the nerve up to ask her. In the morning I stuck my left arm up from the cot that I was lying on. Dave thought I was going to hit him. But I just held my arm there for about 5 minutes, to get back at the boss's brother who found out I was holding my arm up.

Another time we were in Keene, NH. I went out on a date with a girl I met on an internet dating service. She was a teacher. We went on the date, but she wasn't very pretty. I said after supper lets just be friends. I never heard from her again.

But the Budweiser Brewing Co. was there. After the campaign, on the last day of the campaign for that area, I said let's take the Bud factory tour but none of the guys wanted to go in. I figured these stoneheads would want to go on a beer factory tour, but no.

One night we stayed at the boss's uncle's cabin in the woods. It was freezing out, but the cabin had a wood stove. We all slept in there about 10 of us. I had to sleep on the floor below the couch. In the morning I had a problem. The guys said I wasn't going to make it through the day. But I knew God would help me, and he did that day.

Another time we were starting a drive in R.I., and the boss gave me $50, for driving all the tables and chairs to the office in my Nissan. The boss' brother found out and he wanted to beat me up and take the $50. Somehow I got out of it. And the boss told his brother to "knock it off, you're not in high school anymore". I said goodbye to this group after that, and I didn't work for them anymore.

Chapter 24

More Jobs

Then I had my own store on Pleasant St., in Gloucester. It was a sporting goods consignment/hobby store. I got a loan from the bank for $10,000, and me and my father went to Gonsalves toy wholesalers, and we bought $10,000 worth of toys. I had rockets, games, models, train sets, toy army men, matchbox cars, and v64 scale nascar stock cars, Star Trek cards, and action sets of WWII, and the civil war.

But it was also a sporting goods consignment shop. I sold hockey skates, bicycles, and rollerblades. One day a man came who's last name was Laffata (he must have taken a lot of ribbing for that name), brought in 5 or 6 new tennis racquets. I said I can't afford to buy them but he said I could place them on consignment. They never sold. Everyday a kid came in to see if his ice skates had sold. He said he was responsible for getting the CATA bus to go to the mall. I was impressed and I hired him to work the counter sometimes.

One day I sold a bicycle for $100. I was supposed to give $50 to the owner for the consignment price. I don't know what happened, but I spent his $50. So he comes in and demands his money, I didn't have it, so I told him to come back the next day. I had to go to the bank and get $50 out to give him.

Then my friend Bob Store, gave me a cardboard cutout of Worff from Star Trek the next generation for a window display. I had the trainset in the window too. One day all the kids came by the store marching in the street. They were all wearing their baseball uniforms, from the various teams, and they looked at my store front window, and said "Smoking Joe"! That was the name of the train set in my window. I thought these kids liked it, maybe they will buy it, but they didn't.

I had a model competition in the store. But I only had two contestants. They brought in their model tanks and I judged the winner, and gave him a free toy. I can't remember what it was.

One day a gloucester policeman came in the store. He was looking at the WWII, and civil War playsets. I told him the history of the Civil War playset how that the rebels had their best sharpshooters on top of a rock called the Devil's Tower". They were picking off Yankees like no tomorrow. So finally the Yankees fired a lucky cannon shot, into the tower and knocked out the rebs. The police man was appreciative of my story, and he came back the next day and bought it.

I was selling pogs too at the time. The competition, Matt's Sports Plus down the street, was selling pogs for 10 cents each. So I got some and sold them for 5 cents each. I sold a 100 of them. But he made $80,000 on his pogs.

I also sold temporary tattoos. I put a tattoo on a girls belly one day. And then one day some punk kid stole once of my model airplanes. It was worth $40. I told the police, and there was an ad in the police notes the next day.

Then I sold Star Trek the next generation cards to a group of teenage boys. The one kid goes "I feel a Data here". But he didn't get Data. I was new to the Star Trek cards, and I asked the kid if I could see his cards. He said yes, and I was intrigued by the cards, and I looked at them for a couple minutes. Then the kid said "can I have my Star Trek cards back.?" I gave them back to him and he said thank you.

Then one day my stupid uncle Jack, came over to the store and he layed down in the backroom, but he was still visible. A guy came in the store, and saw Jack lying there. So I was like "dam". I had to be super nice to the guy. Then I kicked Jack out. I gave him flyers to put on all the car front windshields to advertise a sale I was running. Everything 25% off. But I think he never passed the flyers out, he rooked me.

So sadly Sports and Hobby Hideaway was no more. I had to fold for lack of business.

Then I worked as bell ringer for the Salvation Army. It was freezing cold, but there I was ringing that bell. Sometimes people would come by and give you hot chocolate or coffee. I only did that one Christmas.

Then I worked at Rule Industries, when the paint factory moved to the Cape Ann Industrial Park. The whole operation was moved to one big room, with gas light for lighting. The wall was lined with chemicals, and there was two lines for filling paint cans, though we only used one line. But there was still chemicals left in the laboratory at the paint factory. Me and another worker were told to fill the barrel with all the powders, and liquids, left in the lab. We poured vial after vial of powders into the 55 gallon barrel. We pretended to be the 3 stooges making a stooges batch. With all the chemicals in there its a wonder they didn't have a reaction and blow up. But I had fun pretending I was Curley, and I was singing "la, la, la, la", as I poured the power into the barrel.

At the end of the day the foreman's boss, drove us from rocky neck to Kondelian Rd., in his labaron convertible. We got chemicals all over our clothes and feet, and got his new car dirty.

So at Rule Industries at: the Cape Ann Industrial Park, I got promoted to paint filler, (E pay). I used to fill those paint cans so fast, the packers couldn't keep up with me. But I showed no mercy. I just kept filling fast.

But I also continued to make the kl concentrate. They moved the tanks with the propeller shafts to a corner of the room. They also had the rosin grinder break. And I challenged the other workers if they could get it cooking by first break.

But soon I left the paint department to work in the shipping dept. It was so much fun. I was a natural born shipper. I had to stock all the paint can boxes in the stock room. Cans of paint were 25lbs. a piece. So box of four was 100lbs. I used to lift them, and stock them, and ship them like they were 10lbs.

So I packed the paint can boxes on pallets for shipping, but soon I was pulling orders for the Boat Zoap, compasses, winches, bilge pumps, and anchors. I had my own desk next to Donna, and Bonnie, my co-shippers.

I used to sit at my desk and add up all the weights of everything and put shipping labels on all the boxes, and put a bill of lading on the top box.

They had an automatic shrink wrapper devise. You put a pallet on the base of the machine, and start the wrapping plastic on one side, and you turn the machine on and it spins round and round and automatically wraps the plastic around the boxes.

They had fork lifts there, I went on a lot. I used to drive the fork lift at full speed through the hallways, with boxes of bilge pumps, on the pallet. I used to wear my head phones on while I was driving, and the foreman saw me and told me not to drive the fork lift with head phones on. That was a bummer.

Soon I worked about two months or so as a shipper, and I didn't realize shippers get (F pay). So I went over everybody's head and told the president of the company that I had been working for two months at (E Pay) money when I should have been making (F pay) money, because the president met with all the workers and said if there's ever a problem at work to see him.

So my boss, Pete Dumas checked his records of my time in the shipping dept. and I got a nice check for $300. I used to do UPS shipping there too. We had to put shipping labels on all the outgoing boxes to put them on a pallet, and when the UPS truck came, I loaded all the boxes on the truck with the UPS guy. I used to pretend that the light boxes were heavy and the heavy boxes were light.

There was also a giant crushing machine that crushed all the cardboard boxes into bundles wrapped with wire • to make a bundle of cardboard, that I put into a trailor truck for safe keeping till the trailor was full.

Donna helped me make a budget of my income. I was able to save around $40/week. I was making around $225/week, and I bought a brand new 1987 Nissan Pathfinder.

That was a great SUV. It made everybody jealous. When we worked at the filling line we wouldn't wear our glasses. But when the foreman's boss came in the room quickly put them on.

One day I had to install the gas lights on the ceiling. We had a step ladder about 20ft. off the floor. We installed the lights but were very high off the ground. I grabbed on to the guy to keep him steady, and myself steady as well. I was scared, but we did it.

Chapter 25
Untitled

After I arrived in gloucester for the summer of 1984, we used to party at the pit. Its just a rock wall, about 50' high. We used to ride our motorcycles to the top around the side. But off to the right is where we used to party. It was a smaller rock formation, with like a 15' rock wall. We had a fire going every Friday night.

We also used to party at the "smoking hole". Just a little gathering area of the woods, by the Joe's Variety store. Every day we would play "match games". Where one guy would light a joint and another guy would match him a joint. It seemed to me I was the only one doing all the matching.

So every Friday night, we would hang out at the store. Me, Bobby Monroe, John Rambert, Paul Temple, Fred Armstrong, Phil Haynes, Brad Williamson, Karate Man Dave, and Paul Silver, and Bobby Colonel, used to hang out at the store, and wait for someone to buy us a beer ball. We always seemed to find a buyer, and Bobby Colonel used to charge $2/ cup. Then we took the beer ball to the pit and get drunk and stoned. The combination of pot and alcohol are called "speed balls". Every night when I got home and lie in bed, I would get bed spin. That's when you lay in bed and the bed would spin around and around. It was both scary and fun.

Then we used to party at my house too. The gang used to throw their beer bottles of the porch, I told them not to. One night my friend Brad, was high on acid, and purposely knocked my motorcycle on its side. Karen Chamberlain brought him home after he had shown remorse for what he had done.

One night everybody slept over at my house. In the morning we woke up to Ozzy and Black Sabbath in concert on Live Aid. The concert put on by Bob Geldorf, for hunger relief in Africa. I got to listen to it at the moonie's that night at work.

Chapter 26
More Jobs

I used to work at Toys R Us too. I was in the stock room. I only worked there about 2 weeks. They had a football pool each week. If you got the most picks right you would win the pool. I never won. But at lunch me and this other guy used to go to the Happy Whale in the mall, and get beer, and fries. I always had a little buzz at work.

Then I used to work driving cab. That was fun. I used to work the over night shift. One night was a great night. We had to drive a large family to Framingham. It took 2 cabs to do it. The guy was stuck in Gloucester with car trouble, so we drove him and his family home to Framingham for $90 apiece.

Another job was working for the Cape Ann Delivery Service. It's a service where you pick up food at restaurants, ordered by customers, then drive it to their house. We had cb radios installed in all the cars. One day the boss, Russ Peres, wanted me and this other guy to get an antenna from a barn on the south shore. The antenna was like 30' of the ground, so we put a ladder up to get it. I climbed about halfway there and chickened out. The other guy didn't want to climb the ladder either. So we said "fuck this", I wasn't going to risk my life for some stupid antenna, and we drove away from their empty handed.

Then I worked with my uncle Dave surf clamming on his 35' novy boat. We had dredge with a big bag on the end to collect the clams. The dredge was dragged off the boom at the stern of the boat. The dredge would dig into the sandy bottom with a hose attached to it, and would disrupt the sand. As the dredge drags along, the clams would get scooped up into the bag. After we dragged for a 1/4 mile we would haul it up and get the clams out, and put them into burlap bags a bushel at a time. We only got like 8 bushels and that was it for surf clamming.

Chapter 27
More Partying Days

So every Friday night was a party at the pit. At the time I was seeing a girl named Laura Lamberchain. She wasn't the prettiest girl in the world, she was on the heavy side, but had tremendous tits. I used to go out with her privately. We hadn't had sex yet but was heavy petting. One Friday night she came to my house and said "you can do anything you want with me". I didn't want my friends at the party to know I was using Laura as a pig, so I coughed and coughed pretending I had a bad cold. So I stayed home from the party that night.

At that time, there was a drive in theater down the street. One week me, and my cousin Stoney, (who was like a god, because he always had weed), and Bobby Monroe watched the movie every night of the week. We sat next to the projection booth, and got stoned. Stoney used to buy an ounce of weed at a time. That summer we smoked Columbian gold everyday. Stoney used to roll 3/4 of the ounce as joints for $2/joint. He made enough money that his 1/4 ounce was free.

One night I was considered worthy to drive around with Stoney and Peter Hawkes. We drove to the combat zone, (a bridge over Essex Ave, by the Little River Mart), and got stoned with like 8 guys, who partied at their woods near the combat zone. I smoked my pot with them and they all worshipped me. Stoney and Peter left me there, because I had betrayed them. We had parties at the pit, and Stoney used to show up, and everybody thought Stoney was so cool because he always had dope.

Chapter 28
My Motorcycle

I bought a 1978 Yamaha DT 175 motorcycle for $300. Bobby Monroe said it was a good deal. He had a 1978 Yamaha DT 125. But my DT didn't run right. Something was making it very slow. My cousin Fred, (Stoney's brother), helped me fix it. I spent $500 fixing it. We put on a new chain, new brakes, new fork oil, Boysen racing reed, new tires, new seat, new handle bars, and throttle grips. But it still didn't run right. So we took it to a Yamaha dealer in N. Reading, and they burnt out the muffler, the baffle. I got on it and fired that thing up and went on a test drive. That thing flew like the wind. I was so impressed by the power. One day we were riding and I passed Bobby Monroe on his 125 like lightning. Bobby never rode with us after that again.

We would all ride our bikes to the cross, and get high. Then ride our bikes to the reservoir, and around to the pipeline.

Stoney used to work at cycles 128 in Beverly, in the parts dept. And one day all his friends from the cycle shop came to our riding group and we all went riding on the pipeline. His friend was riding an atv, and he got stuck. He surprised us all by putting it in reverse gear, and blasted out of the trouble he was in. Me and Stoney looked at each other like "what the fuck"!

One day I beat Stoney on his motorcycle. He had a Suzuki RM 125. I raced him and passed him on the long straightaway around the reservoir that runs parallel to the highway. Then I passed him again on a little circle that was in the woods. He went around it, but I cut across it, and got in front of him. I floored it all the rest of the way without looking back, to the end of the trail. I don't think he liked that.

One night, me and Fred rode our bikes to the candy house on exit 12, rt. 128. We were stuck there, because the police were coming. So we rode our motorcycles down the breakdown lane going south on northbound rt. 128. But we really wanted to lose the police so we continued on to exit 14, got off the highway and floored it to Fernald St. and safety.

We used to ride our bikes down Conomo Point Road. The road had many jumps in it, that was fun going over them. We did a lot of road riding.

One night we rode down to Wingaersheek beach. I accidently rode right into the ocean. My bike stalled and it died. I was stuck at Wingaearsheek beach, luckily Fred gave me a ride on the back of his bike, to my house where I got my truck, a black 1964 Ford F100. And I drove to the beach and picked up my bike on the side of the road and brought it home. Then I immediately took the head off the cylinder, and dumped Marvel mystery oil in the cylinder to save it from the salt water that got in there. Luckily I was able to save it in time, and it started back up.

One day me and Fred rode our bikes to the reservoir, and it was winter. We had a lot of very cold days in a row, and the res was frozen. So we rode our bikes on the frozen lake. Incredibly the ice never broke, and we rode all over that small lake. Then we counted our blessings when we finally made it back to land.

My last adventure with my DT, was in town. I registered the bike and made it street legal. It seemed that the police were picking me up on a lot of traffic stops. So when two state troopers put the blues on me. I was riding. I decide to go for it. I gunned the Yamaha through the rotary and south bound 128. Two state troopers were hot on my tail. I took the exit 12. Causeway St. off the highway. One trooper was right behind me, and the other went on straight on the highway and took exit 13 to cut me off at the corner of Causeway and Concord St. Come to find out he said he would have been able to stop me on the corner, but a little old lady in her car got in the way.

So I made it to the Joe's Variety, and I saw Bobby Monroe, and a couple other friends there. So I was just about to blast it up Beckham Circle, and to the bridal path, but I was afraid the police would go back to the store and ask the kids if they knew me. So I didn't want to take that chance and I gunned it down Concord St. past the Atlantic St. intersection and continued down Concord St. towards the bridal paths southern entrance off Bray St.

So when I got to Bray St. I decided I would really lose the police who were hot on my tail, by keep going down Concord St. to the other Concord St. entrance to the bridal path and the cross. So one trooper stayed with me, and the other trooper went down the Bray St. to cut me off.

So I continued down Concord St. thinking I would blast into the trail and head home, where they would never find me. But I took the wrong trail at the street to the bridal path and met with a security gate. I didn't realize that I wanted the second entrance to the path. So I laid the bike down on the ground, and I just ran into the troopers arms, who had gotten out of his cruiser. He put the cuffs on me, and soon his partner showed up, and they talked about the arrest. All they were going to stop me for was, I didn't have any eye protection on. It probably been just a warning or a small fine. I laughed as they talked about me, because I thought it was funny. They put me in the cruiser. But I slipped the cuffs from behind me and under my feet, and I had my hands cuffed in front of me. When the cop saw me he readjusted the cuffs to go through the seat belt so I couldn't slip them anymore. They towed my bike to Tally's in Gloucester, and I didn't see any jail time. I just paid a de cent fine and got out of there!

Now the very last thing I did on my Yamaha was, I gave my girlfriend, Mary Vault, a ride to work at Friendy's. The bike didn't have an exhaust on it, just little tiny pipe. When I drove her to work, my friends said you could hear me coming all the way from the bridge.

Chapter 29
Mushrooms, and French Girls

All the gang partied in the camp Stella Mara camp ground one night. We were all tripping on magic mushrooms. I ate like a gram. Then Brad knocked the roof of the porch of one building. I was upset for the vandalism but said nothing. It was late at night, and we were up all night, and there was a building there like a great hall. I wanted all of us to sleep in there, for the night, but nobody else did. So we went home in the morning.

One night we went down Old Bray St., and to the back side of the Cape Ann Camp site. We were in the woods and came to the edge of the campsite. And two French girls came over to see us. When they came over, all the gang ran away, frightened. They yelled "come back!" but I stayed there and talked to them.

I learned they were from France, visiting America. But their father who was a stones throw away wouldn't let them out of his sight. And I said goodbye to them.

Chapter 30

The Cars II had in My Life

I had many cars in my life, I'll try to list them all here. But I may forget a couple of them.

My first car was a black 1967 Chevy II Nova. It had a 350 v8, and a four barrel carburetor. That was a real muscle car. I put creager wheels on it and Goodyear eagle tires.

Then my father gave me his 1970 Datsun 240z rally car. It was red with a black hood, and a roll bar in the back. This is the same car he raced in the Canadian winter rally. It had a straight 6 cylinder engine, and it was very fast. It could go 160 mph. The 240z can blow away Mustangs and Camaro's off the line.

Then I bought my sister's white Subaru XT. It has a button you could push on the gear shift, and it went into 4 wheel drive. That was a cool car. I sold it to a guy form NH, who collected XT's.

Then I had a green Chevy Nova, but the trunk never stayed shut. When we drove it the passenger always had to get out and shut the trunk at intersections.

Then I had a 1964 black Ford F100 pick up truck, that I bought for $50. It had a generator that never kept a charge. I always had to keep two batteries in it, so when one went dead, I would hook up the other battery. I had a small business with Fred, as we sold tree logs for firewood. We used to go into the bridal path with my truck, and cut down 4' logs for a truckload of wood, that we sold for $50.

Then I had a white Buick sedan, that I got for $1000. I only had that car for a short while.

Then I had a white 1977 VW Rabbit. It had really cool black pinstriping, and it said "WABBITT" on the front windshield. I traded it in for a brand new 1987 Nissan Pathfinder, silver, with red pinstriping, and a triangle window in the center. It was the first year for Pathfinders. I put the sound system in myself, with an amplifier and speakers that I put in the back seats on the side panels. I used to drive my SUV 85 mph on the highway. It had a v6 3.0 liter engine. I wrecked the front end after I smashed into a van's rear bumper. I gave it back to the dealer.

After that I had a green 1995 Chevy Camaro. It said "I LOVE JESUS" on the windshield. I told the guy when I bought it, that I was not going to take that sign off. That was a cool car.

Then I had a 1988 black Nissan compact truck. The starter didn't work, so I always had to park it on a hill and jump start it. It was probably worth close to a grand, but I sold it for $200 just to get rid of it.

Then I had a 1994 red Ford Ranger compact station wagon. I sold it.

Then I had a 1984 black Audi GT. It was a nice car, but I ran it out of water and blew the engine up and junked it.

After that I bought a 2004 blue Ford F150 truck. I bought it in NH, and I paid for it all in about 1 year later. I loved that truck. Then I got into an accident, and totaled it. I got $3000 for it and my father gave me a 1995 red Ford Ranger pickup truck, and I put $2500 into it fixing it up. But I couldn't drive it because it wouldn't pass inspection, because the bumper was rotted off.

So my father gave me a black 1994 GMC Sierra, pick up truck. That was the last vehicle that I owned. I cannot drive anymore due to my illness, and I sold that truck for $1200. It had a cap that I forgot about, and the guy who bought it, saw it, and I gave it to him for free. The truck has a cassette player in it, and I threw in a couple cassettes as a bonus. The cars greatest hits, and WOW 1998 Christian artists. That was all the cars I owned.

Chapter 31

My Conversion to Christ

In the summer of 1986 we were in the smoking hole getting stoned. And I felt the urge to leave. So I told Bobby Monroe I was leaving the gang. I wanted to stop smoking pot, and come to Jesus. It was time for me to grow up. I was 20 and for my birthday, I went to the Cape Ann Bible Church, and grabbed the pastor (Walter Ross), afterwards and said "I want to get saved." So we went into a back office at the church, and he said something and I prayed, and I knew I was "born again"!

I had received Christian witness from several sources at Russell High School in KY. I used to steal comic books from Chick Publications from the library and read them. They were a strong witness to me. Other classmates told me about Jesus, but I wasn't ready yet. They must have been praying for me.

So after church I got in the car of my waiting grandmother, and put the music on. It was rock music and I knew it was wrong, right there, so I said "nanny do you think we should turn the radio off?" Today I still like rock music, but I am careful as to what I am listening to. For example when I hear "I'm on the highway to hell" by ACDC, I know it's time for me to change the station. Or Van Halen's "running with the devil" it's time for me to change the station.

So I found Jesus or should I say Jesus found me. Soon I was going to men's bible study at church. And I liked Jimmy Swaggert on tv. He kept saying you had better go to a church where the Spirit of God was flowing. That made me think. At bible study I relayed this information to the pastor. The Spirit of God was at that church, you could feel the Spirit in the songs they sung. But they didn't believe in the gifts of the Spirit, like speaking in tongues, and prophesy, and healing by the laying on of hands.

But I was going to present the speaking in tongues to the bible study, but the pastor wouldn't let me. He said "that's Armenian." He subscribed to the Calvinist view of tongues. For the real educated student of the bible there is a thing called "the TULIP", where each letter stands for something, but I can't remember what.

So then I was going to Gloucester Assembly of God church, because I wanted to go to a church where the Spirit of God flows. AOG is a Pentecostal church, and they believe in speaking in other tongues.

It's called the second experience in God in Pentecostal circles. You get saved by the blood of Jesus, but then you persue the baptism in the Holy Ghost, with the evidence of speaking in other tongues. The baptism makes you come alive in Christ, with the gifts and the fruit of the Spirit. It gives you power to live for Jesus. "You can't live the Christian life, you have to ask Jesus to live it for you".

So at work (Rule Industries) I was going around and saying "Jesus Loves You!" to everybody. And I was happy at work. I used to sit by myself and listen to Wayne Monbleu's show let's talk about Jesus" show on AM radio. At 2nd break I used to sit by myself at my desk and just read the Psalms and the New Testament. When I got home from work every day, I would put it on Jimmy Swaggerts show 'A Study in the Word". You could feel the anointing of the Spirit right through the television set.

But one day at work, I was stocking paint boxes in the stock room, and two of the guys said "Hey Jesus Loves You"! to get my attention. And they said "you know everything thinks you're an asshole going around saying that." So I said "I don't care what everybody thinks about me, I'd rather care what God thinks says about me." And their jaws dropped, as they stood there stunned. And with that I went back to work.

I used to witness to Diana, and Vicky. Diana kept saying I was reborn, but I had to correct her saying I was "born again." I used to say to Vicky, "Vicky, you need to let go and let God."

I used to listen to Stryper cassettes while stocking paint. I swear after hearing Stryper's song "Stand Up and Fight", I wanted to kill somebody. One day I was walking into the stock room, and there was a man in there working. I said "repent", as I walked by him. Then my friend Johnny McDougal wanted to get close to God and he said "I prayed while I was in the John" I said "that's great that you prayed. But you prayed while you were going to the bathroom." "God deserves better than that." He later married Vicky. Vicky had huge boobs. And she showed me her cleavage and half her boobs, after Jimmy said its alright. I wanted to see them again, but said nothing.

Chapter 32
Holly

About this time I started dating a girl named Holly Utopia. She was my aunt's, cousin's, daughter, or something like that. So I called her on the phone, and asked her out. She said yes, and I went over to her house. We went out in my Pathfinder, to a wooded side road. We hopped in back and she gave me felatio. After, I said "do you want to be sorry"? Realizing I had just sinned against God. Later by myself I asked God to forgive me, and he did.

But soon I was having sex with Holly everyday. I was allowed to sleep over at her parents' house. Her bedroom was on one side and my bedroom, was on the other. She had a waterbed that was always warm, even in summer. She could snake around that bed like a cobra, and slide around the satin sheets. Every night I would go into her bedroom, make love to her, and go back to my bedroom. And I would ask God to forgive me for having sex, and he did. Then I prayed that she wouldn't get pregnant every night too.

In the morning we had cereal, and she went to work with her mother, to the hotel, where she was a chambermaid. And I would drive my Pathfinder to work from Billerica about 40 miles to Rule Industries.

Later I found out that she didn't want to have sex every night, but I thought she wanted me to.

So we made love everywhere, at her house, at my house, on the lookout rock, or a bale of hay in my basement, at Howard Johnsons, in Burlington.

One night she said to me "you don't want me, I am nothing but a little slut". But I did want her, I loved her. We went to the mall in NH, I wanted to buy her the entire mall. We started out looking for a leather jacket for me, and ended up buying a fur coat for her.

At Howard Johnsons she wanted to prove to me she was just a little slut. I bought her a white Russian, at this little diner, and we went to the hotel. We had sex all night long, til past 5am in the morning. We took a bath, and I shampooed my hair into devil's horns, she got scared. So we left at the checkout time the next day.

Then we took a trip to NYC, in my Pathfinder. That night we tried to find a hotel room, but we couldn't. This one place I saw was $50 for one hour. It was a prostitute hotel, so we went across the bridge to NJ, and found a room for $50 for one night. The room had a mirror on the ceiling above the bed. The next morning I prayed for forgiveness for having sex again. He forgave me.

So we went to the Statue of Liberty, and climbed the stairs to the top of the lady and looked out. Then we took the ferry back to the mainland, from Ellis Island. And it was cold, and we were cold, and running out of money, so we bought matching sweatshirts, to keep us warm, and had lunch.

Then we went to the World Trade Center's twin towers. And we went to the top. Then she went to the bathroom, and I couldn't find her and I was scared. Finally she came out. I would have been lost without her. Then we went back to my Pathfinder, where I got a parking ticket, that I never paid to this date. That night we left NY and pulled the SUV into a highway park and ride lot. That night I had to keep starting the truck up to get heat because we were cold. We made love the next morning in the back of the SUV. People who were taking the shuttle bus, saw us naked in the SUV, it must have made their day.

So my sexual activities with Holly continued for three months. But then I began to feel sorryful sinning against God so many times, that I wanted to breakup with her. Its the kindness of God that leads you to repentance. You can only engage in sinful activity for so long, when the mercy and grace of God, pulls you into a right relationship with him again.

She couldn't get over it, and swallowed 19 contact pills. So I rushed her to the hospital, and they gave her charcoal to swallow. She puked the pills and her life was saved. But I just thought to myself this girl was ready to die for me, I can't breakup with her.

So the sex continued for another 3 months. We went to my aunt's cabin in ME, and we got lost driving there. It was just a miracle that we pulled up along side her mother's car and aunt Fran, at a light. And we followed them to the cabin.

That night we saw a guy, who was my aunt's friend, and he stayed over too. But I broke the rules of man to woman sex, by not checking in with this guy first about our relationship. And Holly made love to me, that night in the loft. It was the best sex we ever had. In the morning I took a shower, and immediately after that, my heart hurt. I had broken the rules of normal man to woman sex. And my heart really hurt and I was going to cry out, but I just shucked my emotions, and took it.

So we all went x-country skiing at a x-country ski resort in ME. But rather than skiing which would have been fun, we bought matching sweatpants that said Maine on the side of them.

So our relationship came to an end one night. She was at my grandmother's house and I was at my house, just 200 yards away. And I talked to her on the phone. When I hung up, I began thinking. (She's down there, I'm up here. She's down there, I'm up here, she's down there, I'm up here.) So I ran down the street to see her. I felt a little foolish running past my friend Happy Jack's house. But I wanted to break all the rules.

So I ran down to see her, and when I got there she met me there, but she didn't let me in. So I ran to other side and got to the sliding glass door, but she got there first and locked it. So I kicked the side of the house, and went back to the front door. I would have asked her to marry me, I wasn't sure. But at this time her mother and my aunt Fran came home. So I met them and they were trying to see what's going on. So rather stick up for myself, I let her get away with her games. She came out and teased me by hiking her dress over her knee.

So I left her at the driveway and walked home with my mother. But I walked on the wrong side of my mother. Instead of walking on her left I walked on her right. Holly saw this from the car she was in. And I was gonna go back and confront her once more, but instead I walked home with my mother on her right side.

The next day I was in bed and I wanted Holly. My mother came in my room and I said "where is she, I want her". I thought my mother could magically make her appear. And my mother said to me in a strange voice "this is what you want?" I was like "Yeah" but said nothing. Later on that night and for a long time after that I had to clutch my pillow, to pretend it was her with me in bed.

So we were officially broken up. But we still had sex a couple times later. We went to my grandparents 50th wedding anniversary at the legion in Gloucester. All my cousins were there. And Holly was there and she was getting drunk, and I was getting drunk. Then our song came on the room. It was the song 'Take My Breathe Away' by Berlin, that was a song we made love to. It was our song, and magically it came over the floor, and I fell on my knees and I laid my head on her lap. All my cousins were looking on saying to themselves "what's going on here?" So me and Holly danced, but she was still playing games, by saying this is our only dance. So I took her, and it was all I could do to keep us both standing up as we danced, because we were both drunk.

So I took her home in my SUV, and when I opened the trunk there was a knife in the car. I don't know how it got there, but it was there. I didn't put it there, and my cousin Andrea was worried that I would carve Holly up, but I would never do that. So she let me drive her home. At my house Holly puked up all the ravioli she had eaten in the bathroom. Instead of making her throw up in the toilet, I let her throw up in the sink, and we laid down in my mother's bed. Then Holly's mother came to pick her up, and I helped her to the car. I gave her mother all Holly's panties that were in my bureau. So that was it. I only saw Holly couple times after it was all over. And we made love but the spark was gone.

Everyday at work, I would think about her, and think about her, everyday. Then one day I finally stopped thinking about, and I got back into my life with Jesus.

Chapter 33
Rule and The Day I Quit

So at work, at Rule, strange things began happening. I was flirting with the girls there, and would have started a new relationship with a girl but I was too stupid to go along with her. So at work I began doing things weirdly. They put me in the bilge pump dept. which was no where near fun as the shipping dept., and I was stacking the boxes on the pallet weirdly.

So one day I was asking my co-worker Penny, a lot of questions about women. I wanted to know what made them tick. So I asked her all kinds of questions, and she answered them all. Then I heard a voice say "leave". So I went to the bathroom to hang out for about 5 minutes. I came back to work and the voice said "I said leave". So I thought it was the voice of God and I told the foreman Ralph that I wanted to quit. So I left my cigarettes with Penny, and went outside to my Pathfinder. But along the way I was thinking (I don't want to quit, how am I going to pay for my Nissan?) But I was thinking this is the will of God for me. I didn't say goodbye to any of the guys, I just forsook everyone and I quit. Thinking this is God's will for me. But with God you can get it right or you can get it oh so wrong. I got it "oh so wrong". This was the beginning of my mental illness.

Chapter 34
Israel

The last thing I did at Rule before I quit was go on vacation. And I took a trip to Israel.

MY TRIP TO ISRAEL by John Banner

The year was 1987-Easter time. I was working at Rule Industries when I took my vacation from work – seven days with a weekend on each end. So, I was a Christian and decided to go to Israel. My father is a retired commercial airline pilot for TWA so kids fly free, up to 21 years old. So, I was 20 years old and I had better go somewhere for free fast-before I was to lose the opportunity to fly free forever.

So I took a flight from Boston's Logan Airport to New York's JFK airport to Tel Aviv Israel. I was flying standby, the flight was full and I couldn't get on. That's what you do when you fly stand by; you stand there watching your plane take off and you wave bye-bye. When I got to New York I had to kill three days before the next flight to Tel Aviv was scheduled. I stayed at the New York YMCA. I can't remember what I did there. I didn't do anything special; I kind of just wandered the streets.

I finally got back to JFK airport and my flight to Tel Aviv, Israel. I sat in first class. I witnessed to the guy next to me; shared the gospel with him and planted some seeds. He said I wouldn't like where he was going - he was going to a nudist colony somewhere. Flying to Tel Aviv is boring. There is nothing to see but water. Water is everywhere. All of a sudden you see the Mediterranean Sea and you see dry land for about five minutes, then you land in Tel Aviv. When we landed I looked out the window and I couldn't believe my eyes - there were soldiers with machine guns. I thought "Well, we're not in Kansas anymore, Jimmy" and "I hope they don't shoot me". I got my duffel bag at baggage claim, the tiny lock I had on it was still secure, so thank God.

I was told by my mother's rector at St. John's Episcopal Church to look for a ride called the "sherute". It's just a big, eight passenger Mercedes Benz. It was supposed to take me to my hotel in Jerusalem. So, I found the "sherute" and we made the half-hour journey to Jerusalem and to my hotel, the Jerusalem YMCA. The archway on the front door says "Everlasting Father, Mighty God, Prince of Peace, and Wonderful Counselor".

I got to my hotel at dark; it was $30 a night. Anxious to start exploring the old city Jerusalem, I put on my head phone (I was listening to Janet Paschal) and walked by the front desk. The clerk looked at me like typical American, so I went through the back alleys that lead to the Jaffa gate. I was hoping I wouldn't get mugged. I went to the Jaffa gate and started exploring. There were many shops still open. A little t-shirt stand had a cool t-shirt that had jet fighters on it and the slogan said, "Don't worry America, Israel will protect you!" I bought one for my friend - I should have bought one for myself as well. I walked the narrow cobblestone street to the heart of the old city; gold was being sold everywhere. Lots of bling, bling! So, I saw pretty much for now, and I went back to the Y.

The next day was Easter. I heard the service going on in a building adjacent to the front door of the Y. I was going to join them when all of a sudden "jet lag" hit. It was day light here, but, it was night time back in the States. I was exhausted and had to crash.

The next day I joined seven or eight people on a walking tour with a local historian as guide. We walked around to various places of interest inside the old city. Then we came to a place where the guide said Jesus was once arrested. Apparently, according to history, Jesus was arrested more than once. I left the group, not because of that, but because I felt like leaving the walking tour.

So, I explored the old city some more. The old city Jerusalem is made up of four quarters: The Christian quarter, the Armenian quarter, the Jewish quarter and the Muslim quarter. While in the Christian quarter I visited the shrine of the holy sepulcher. This is where Catholics believe Jesus was buried in his tomb. There was a long line waiting to go in. I stayed there a little longer than most people... some assumed I was really religious. Then I made my way to the western wall of the temple - the "wailing wall". I put my prayer on a piece of paper and shoved it in a crack in the wall, like the Jews would do. Tourists were looking at me as odd. But, I just thought "when in Rome..."

Next, I rented a car, a very small Suzuki, and I went to Mount Masada and the Dead Sea. I stopped at Qumran, the place where they found the "dead sea scrolls". I explored a cave, and from there saw the Dead Sea. I drove down to the sea but didn't go swimming in it. At Mount Masada I took the gondola up, and explored the top. History says the Jews who were up there were trying to escape from the Romans. The Jews had baths and plenty of water while the Romans had none. The Jews taunted the Romans by dumping water over the side of the mountain and laughing at them. Rome could not get up there. Finally Rome had enough, and with Roman ingenuity built a huge ramp to the top of the mountain, to get the Jews. So, the Jews, rather than fall into the hands of the Romans, committed suicide. After I checked out the mountain, I trekked down Mount Masada.

I drove the Suzuki back to Jerusalem, picking up a hitchhiker along the way, and shared the gospel with him. Back in new city Jerusalem I met a guy, I forget under what circumstances, and we became friends. We picked up his friend, and drove around new city Jerusalem. I was looking for a particular hotel because they had a model of the old city in the lobby. We drove the car to the Jewish quarter and through a small gate that goes through David's citadel, and Mount Zion. Pretty cool! When we departed for the last time, he said to me "You stick with Jesus and I'll stick with God" and I said "All right, I'll pray for you, bye".

Next, I decided to go on a guided tour; so I went on a day trip in a huge Mercedes, eight passenger vehicle. All the taxis in Israel are Mercedes

Benz. There were six of us in the car as we drove to the river Jordan. You can still get baptized there today.

Then we saw the place of the Sermon on the Mount from a distance. There is some kind of shrine there now. Everywhere Jesus was is a shrine! We went to a fifth century synagogue. While checking it out, God put it on my heart to give a lady in the group a flower. I don't know why; but, I just obeyed, snapped off a flower and gave it to her. Then we went to the Sea of Galilee. It's not really a sea; it's more like a large lake. On the shore of this stormy sea was a "tourist trap" stop. I wanted to get a burger, but had no more money since mine was back at the Y. So, the lady I gave the flower to bought me a hamburger. That's why God told me to give her a flower. Praise god! Small miracle, very small.

We took a boat across the Sea of Galilee while our tour guide drove around and met us on the other side. We met at Tiberius. Tiberius is all water slides now. The tour continued as we drove on the west bank. The guide put the stereo on - what do I hear? The Scorpions. I couldn't believe it! The Scorpions were playing on the radio in Israel! I can't remember what song it was, but it was definitely the Scorpions. Anyways, we picked up this Israeli commando hitchhiking. He had his uzzi with him when he got into the car. I didn't dare turn around to look at him. Finally, we dropped him off and I breathed a sigh of relief. But, then we saw tanks on maneuvers. Tanks guarding the border - a giant chain link fence with razors on top. This was serious stuff here! And, that was the end of my guided tour.

I hired this Muslim guy to take me to Bethlehem. We got on the bus for the 15-20 minute ride to Bethlehem. I saw the place where Jesus was born. The Catholics really got in there and catholicized it! The Muslim guy I hired, of course, knew all the store owners there. He led me into the stores and wanted me to buy something. But, I didn't want to buy a wooden elephant so I bought a Coke. Then we took the bus back to Jerusalem. The guide showed me the Temple Mount and the Dome of the Rock. It's the third most holy site to Muslims. I was going to go inside, but you have to take your shoes off. I was afraid someone would steal my shoes, so I didn't go in. I paid the man more than what he was worth, and said goodbye to him.

Then I walked through the Muslim quarter and bought a wicked cool map of the old city. It was irreplaceable; but I have since lost it! For all my friends back home I bought 30 small wooden crosses with the word Jerusalem on them. I walked the Via Delarosa, where Jesus carried his cross. It was very exciting walking this street! If this street could talk. The street ends at the Beautiful Gate and Mount Calvary where Jesus was crucified. Then I saw the Garden Tomb. It's a very solemn place. At the Garden Tomb they have stations where, using paper brochures, you are asked "Wouldn't you like to give your life to Jesus?"

Next, I went to the Mt. of Olives where Jesus will return; where He splits the eastern sky; and every eye shall see Him. It's got an excellent view of the old city with the new city as a back drop behind it. I petted a camel, and then walked to the nearby Garden of Gethsemane. This is where it all came together for me. This is where Jesus put it all on the line. This is where He agonized in the garden knowing what He had to face - the cross. But He said "Not my will be done, but the Father's will be done". This is where Jesus became real for me. This is where I really contemplated Jesus and what He did for me...and where... and how...and why...and when. I loved Him even more. Then I saw the Chapel of the Ascension. It's just a clay hut, but this is where Jesus rose back up to heaven.

I explored the upper room and King David's tomb. You can spend two days in the old city and not get bored! If you go there I recommend that you walk the ramparts walk first. It is just a walkway on top of the wall of the whole old city. By the time you're done walking around the ramparts walk, you will be chomping at the bit to get down there and start exploring.

The last couple nights, I started running out of money, so I had to switch hotels. I left the YCMA, and went to a hotel called the New Imperial Hotel. It's just a stone's throw from the Jaffa gate. It was only $10 a night. The rooms were nice but they didn't have hot water. My last night, I was in the hotel lobby and they had the TV on watching wrestling. I couldn't understand a word they were saying, but there was no doubt they were watching Andre the Giant against two other guys. So I watched a little bit with them; they were amazed an American was watching to with them.

The next day I flew back to JFK and turned my money back into US dollars. You don't get much back when you exchange it to US. Then I went home. THE END.

Chapter 35
Stupid Dr. Ritzkrak

So I continued to live at my mother's house. My mother says "I Love You" in detrimental way. My mother says "I" love you, not, I love "You" Do you see the subtle difference? My mother has selfish love. One day my mother thought it would be a good idea if I went to see her psychiatrist, Martha Norton, who had an office in Gloucester. And my mother said "it's alright John, you can say anything you want to her." "She's a psychiatrist." So I went to one meeting and said nothing, feeling like a dope because I had nothing to say. But I knew this is totally wrong.

So one day my mother saw me in her house watching tv. And she decides there is something wrong with me. So she takes me to the French Center, an old office building, connected to the Addison Gilbert hospital, now torn down for parking space.

So I sat in a meeting with Dr. Ritzkrak, a psychiatrist, and after I told him my personal thoughts, and my personal feelings, he decides something is wrong with me. He has me step out of the room for a second, and he said "I have to" in a funny way, and I realized he was using my "I" that I just told him. He calls me back in the room, and about 10 minutes later, 2 Gloucester cops, very nervous, approached the door, and said "Oh we have to take you away.

If it was alright for the Dr. to use my "I's" in speech, why wasn't it alright for me to keep and say in my own thoughts and feelings? Not hurting anyone, and at peace with the world.

Chapter 36
The Arbor

So the cops took me away to Arbor hospital in Jamaica Plain, MA, on the way I wondered (why am I being taken away?). I have done nothing wrong, and I came to the conclusion that they were going to have sex with me. As we got closer to Jamaica Plain, I started seeing black girls, and I thought (this is gonna be kinky).

Then we were at a traffic light and it turned green. I had to tell the cop to go. "Yeah who's crazy?" He can't even go at a traffic light. So we went to the Arbor, and I went in the door with the cops, and had to sign in. We were at the door and I took 6 steps to the desk to meet the secretary, and signed myself in. If I had known my rights I never would have signed myself in, and this joy ride with the cops would have had me riding back to Gloucester with them.

But I signed in and began with the first of many hospitalizations. My doctor was Dr. Bordeasol, and I wanted to see her but she was no where to be found. They showed me to my room, and I studied it and rather than sit on the bed, I sat on the window ledge, in the back of the room. A black attendant came in and said "John isn't the bed good enough for you?" I just wanted to blow his mind, but said nothing.

Next I was trying to meet the people who were in the hospital with me. So we were in a common area, with a tv., and I looked at the guy next to me on my left, and he goes" what are you looking at"? I should have popped him but said nothing. Then I met a guy who kind of watched out for me. He said it was important that I flexed my muscle around there, so he had me arm wrestle every guy in there. I beat them all. This guy was in the room next to me, we shared a bathroom. He had me write to his daughter with a picture he showed me of her. She was beautiful and I sent her a letter. I was thinking this is why God wants me at the Arbor, to meet my future wife. But it never played out. The guy scared me one night when he came through the shared bathroom and into my room, saying stuff to me about the staff. He scared me man to man, out of my comfort zone between myself and other guys. But I brushed it off and felt better.

So two weeks went by and I didn't see the doctor. I was still trying to figure out why I am in this place. I am not crazy at all. What was the reason I was in here. So time passed and they put me in another unit, not locked. I made a friend, and we talked outside on the grounds. We planned my escape. He gave me $10 for a cab ride. So I threw my bag out the window of my room. Then I crawled on my hands and knees past the nurses station and opened the door, and I escaped. I got on my feet past the door and went down the stairs and pretended I was just a normal everyday person, and I made it outside and picked up my bag, and called a taxi. He took me to the north station, where I caught the train to back to Gloucester.

I got off at the West Gloucester train station and walked home. Then surprise mom, "I'm home".

Chapter 37
Agh and Webber II

A couple days later my mother called the police and the EMT's on me. They said I have to go with the EMT's or the police. So I went with the EMT's to Addison Gilbert hospital's Webber II Unit. During the initial intake interview, they kept asking me "what are you here for?" I kept saying "I don't know", which was true. So they put me on a room program for two weeks. I could not have any stimulation, no tv, no radio, and limited human connection. I was allowed smoke breaks in the little smoking room. The smoking area was where everyone had privacy from the staff, and we all shared our problems. I smoked Camel lights because they tasted so good. I tried to get everyone to smoke Camel Lights so I could bum them of them.

I met a friend Bobby Mercury. The staff used to call us the John and Bob show. We used to be like electricity between us. I used to go to his room and sing Led Zepplin's "whole lotta love." And then quickly leave.

They had five levels and I was on level five. So that meant I could go on unsupervised walks on the hospital campus, which included going between the little variety store and the old mills. But I was the only one on level five so I had no one to walk with me.

Every morning we started the morning with a group, and everyone would talk about how good they slept the night before. Then they talked about their goals for the day. And they started to find different medicines for me. I tried Navane, Thorizane, and Serentil. But finally settling on Clozaril. And I prayed with the councilor "God may this fucking little pill work," and he said "amen". I know it was a bad prayer, but at least he said 'amen.' So they diagnosed me with schizophrenia and the Clozaril worked. It was like a wonder drug. It was like I didn't have schizophrenia at all. So I just went along for the ride, and I spent 2 months at Webber II and was released.

Chapter 38
Danvers State

But my mental health problems weren't over yet. As again I was committed to Danvers State Hospital. But I saw the judge first, and he said I had to do two months there. So they led me out of the court room, and into a little waiting area, with benches. So they handcuffed me to the armrest of the bench, like a common criminal. I had done no wrong. Why am I being handcuffed? So there was like 4 other guys there, all handcuffed to the benches. They were crooks and told me "you'll do two months fast". And they fed us a submarine sandwich, which you had to eat with one hand.

So they brought us by police car to Salem Jail. And they didn't know what to do with me, so they put me in the jail along with the criminals. I was like (Why am I being held behind bars with criminals) But I said nothing out of fear the guys might beat me up. There was a five gallon bucket in the middle of the cell for a toilet. But if you had to go you had to go in front of everybody.

But soon I was taken to Danvers State Hospital. At the initial interview room they questioned me. Then they led me to an exam room, and made me lie down on a table. Then they scratched my feet with a kind of brush, and I made my left foot feel the brush in a funny way. So I took the pain of the test on my left foot. This was key because I had to face these guys, a room full of men. So I stood there and I had to turn around. But I didn't know which way to turn. (do I turn around going left or turn around going right.?') So if I turned left I would have had all the praise from the men. But I turned right, having already experienced the pain on my left. So I turned right feeling my fight was with the women in my head. So I did the two months quickly and got out of there. But I wasn't done yet.

Chapter 39
Webber II Round 2

So I had to go back to Webber II at AGH. They put me on the room program again. No stimulation for two weeks. So I met a councilor there named Sal. And we talked and I told him a lot of personal stuff. And he had me write a story about my left side and my right side. And I wrote my story about my left side, saying its me receiving the world. And I was going to write the story about my right side, saying that's how I reach out to the world, but I was released before I could write the second story.

But I met a girl in there named Beth Daisy. We became friends, even dated a little after our hospitalizations. One day we were at lunch, in the milieu area, and she sat across from me. And I bit into a cherry tomato on purpose, so that the juice would fly across the table and hit her. So I bit down on the little cherry tomato, and the juice flew across the table in a spurt and hit her right in the face. Sal saw it and marveled, just thinking this is just an accident. You had to be there.

So I had my birthday in there and got a half gallon of chocolate ice cream.

But one of the councilors took me under her wing, and really worked with me. She taught me a lot about life. We used to go on walks to the Gloucester Marine, near the hospital. And she said life is not magical, but when I got out of there I found life was magical.

But something was wrong with my hand. It couldn't grasp reality. One day Mary saw there was something wrong with my hand, the way I was holding it. And she said "the hand again" I said yes, but I wanted to say "not the hand, but my hand". But I said nothing. That little phrase would have saved my hand from future problems.

One day one of the patients called Mary out, saying "you think you're something special, don't you". I was happy someone was giving it to the staff. But I felt bad for Mary because she really helped me a lot.

Me and Beth used to talk in the smoking room. And we had rooms across the hall from each other, and we would sit cross legged on the floor, each in our separate rooms, facing each other and talking.

I had the game Axis and Allies there and me and 3 other guys played it. My team won. Then I played it with another guy there. Then I played it with one of the councilors.

One day they were asking me a lot of questions, and in my mind I closed my eyes for a second and said "urine". Later on in my room, in the corner, it smelled like urine, and they asked me if I had peed there, and I said no. This was just the beginning of I had powers. One time while visiting my father in KY, I was driving through Ashland, and I was thinking there needs to be an accident, and I caused it to happen. A UPS truck collided with a passenger car at the intersection. The driver quickly went for the packages that were strewn around, not seeing if the other person was alright.

Just an example of my powers, it seemed like every person I witnessed to about the Lord, died soon thereafter. I preached to my cousin Mark Newman, and he died, I preached to a guy who was staying at my mother's house, and he died, I preached to a guy named Jack, at Happy Jack's house and he died, then I preached to Nancy Biba and she died, then I was sitting in a class in college, and I was like "what's gonna happen now?" Then one of my classmates announced that an author we were studying died. People were dropping dead all around me. But I digress.

So I had my birthday while I was in Webber II. My father, mother, and sister were there. They brought me a cake and chocolate ice cream. Then I overheard one of the councilors talk to my father saying "did you ever hit him," talking about me. And I didn't hear my father's reply, but he never hit me growing up just once or twice.

One day a couple came in to see everybody. They had a guitar and started playing gospel songs. The staff quickly shut them down.

My final day there I said goodbye to everybody, and to two guys especially. One knew I was gonna go to Salem State College, for communications major. And he sang to me Led Zepplin's "communication break down", because he didn't know what else to say. So the other guy was expecting me to say something to him to make boundaries right, but I said nothing. Then as I was about to leave I could have cleared the air right there by saying to the fat girl "and you take your medicine" but I said nothing and walked away.

That boundary bothered me for many years after that. Finally there was a sign on the wall by the door leading out that said "Webber II stops here" I felt like ripping that sign off the wall and keeping it. But I left it there, and said goodbye for the last time at Webber II

Chapter 40

Danvers State Again

So I got committed again to Danvers State Hospital, for two months. They had a ping pong table there, and I played against a black guy named Anthony. We were in the shower area, and I was done showering and Anthony accused me of taking his clothes, which I didn't but got blamed by him anyway. The shower water wasn't hot enough. It was only lukewarm. So I complained, but my complaints fell on deaf ears.

One day I met a friend. He was in his 50's, and he said he was a virgin. He was Catholic and he wanted to see the pope, and ask questions about Catholicism.

We were all in the cafeteria one day, and this guy started choking. He immediately went to the councilor and turned around. The councilor did the Heimlich maneuver on him, and the food popped out of his mouth. Its kind of neat to see the Heimlich done.

Then one of the councilors brought us to the gymnasium, about 9 of us. And I did a half court shot with the basketball, and I threw it one handed over my head, and it went in. It was truly a one in a million shots.

Finally came the day of my release. I had to meet all my doctors, nurses, and councilors at a conference table. The nurse was in a bad mood, and was angry. I was about to say "If you don't like your job, find a new one". But I said nothing, fearing if I said something, they wouldn't let me go. So I quickly listened to their advice for me, and they let me go. That was the last time at Danvers State.

Chapter 41

Jesus Continued

But my love for Jesus never failed. I continued to go to church each Sunday. But then I got introduced to cocaine by neighbor "Happy Jack".

I was trying to party at Jack's house when my stupid mother would knock on the door, and demanding that I come home. I told her to go away so I could party with Jack and his roommates.

We used to go to Lynn and buy $50 packages of coke, and then we would drive all the way back to Gloucester, snort it up and drive all the way back to Lynn for another $50.

But then we cooked it and started doing crack cocaine. One hit and you're an instant addict. We had a pipe we made out of a toilet paper roll, with a hole cut in the top of it, and aluminum foil with pin pricks in it for a bowl, and filled with cigarette ash to smoke it.

Jack would violently shake his arms in front of him. I thought he was going to have a heart attack. He did so much cocaine it burnt a hole in his septum in his nose, and had one big nostril instead of two. I continued to get high on coke once in a while. Then one day I brought Jack to church. But we smoked a joint before we went inside. I couldn't say "let's wait til after church to smoke this". But we got high and went to church. While in there I didn't know what to do so Jack said "sing". And I did. It's a good thing God didn't kill me for doing that.

So we went home and every day we did crack cocaine. I spent my SSI check on it like $600/month, on coke. I was still a Christian but struggled with cocaine addiction. Everyday we did coke, at Happy Jack's house, and drink beer, and get high. I used to cut Jack's lawn for money.

Chapter 42

Hillcrest

So then I got accepted at Hillcrest house, after my hospitalizations. It's a halfway house for people who are dual diagnosed. That is drug addiction and mental illness. It's a very large house with a kitchen and a large dining room table, living room with a tv, and another smaller living room with a tv. Then 3 floors, 3 bathrooms, a basement, and 8 bedrooms. I was on the top floor, with a view of the street, and pond.

I was a Christian, and they let me go to bible study in lua of going to AA meetings. I used to go every Wednesday. But I didn't mess it up for the next guy who came along claiming to be Christian. I left a strong Christian witness there. Used to bake chocolate cakes. One day I was baking a cake and listening to Black Sabbath on cassette. The director called me a hypocrite after that, because of that music. So I shut it off and to this day I don't listen to Black Sabbath.

Everyday at the end of the day when we all got back from program, I would listen to "talk back with Bob Larson" on AM radio. He was a preacher who used to cast out demons from people right over the airwaves. I used to listen with the charge nurse, on the third floor, as she poured out all the medications. So I was witnessing to her via the radio broadcast.

On weekends I used to go out with my friends, Glen Myers, and Craig Rune, and Joshua Miko. We used to go Country Billiards on rt. 1

in Danvers. Then we went in Glen's van, and I was the designated driver. We had like 3 or 4 girls in the van too. We went to the bar and everyone drank but me. I think I had 1 beer, then I was the designated driver.

So I was behind the wheel and we were going through town, and as we drove I was becoming more aware of myself. It was like driving through time. But we went to a bar, and sat at a round table. Everyone was seated nicely, but I had to sit with my back to the bar, and I was like "can someone with a normal brain sit here". Then they would drop me off at Hillcrest, and I said goodbye.

Then I moved out of Hillcrest to an apartment with my friend "orange". We were only living there about a week when for some reason, I don't know what, he stabbed my waterbed with a knife, and threw my chocolate cake on it. Luckily I had a kind neighbor, who helped me drain the waterbed out the window with a hose.

Chapter 43

John

But I continued to do coke, and me, and Happy Jack, and Phil Haynes, and Kevin Haynes, used to go to Lynn, "Lynn, Lynn, the city of sin, you never come out the way you went in." To get coke. Then we would drive back to Happy Jack's house and smoke crack cocaine.

But we would go to this guy's house "Butchie" from Lynn, a black guy, and he would get the coke for us. Then we would give him a small rock, of our coke. One day I gave him a big, nice, piece of rock, and I kind of witnessed to him by using reverse psychology. It made him think twice about what he was doing.

So I met this black guy there, John. He was a big dude. And we became kind of friends. He could score pot for me. But he used to prey on my mental illness. I could never stand up for my own rights.

I had an apartment over the Action Shelter, in Gloucester. And he would sleep on the couch, there. But one day my uncle Dave came by, and John went and hid himself in the closet. He didn't want my family to know he was staying there, so he could manipulate me. So Dave came over and I was about to say "there's a black man in my closet", but I said nothing, thinking John might be a little scared hiding in my closet. So Dave left and John appeared.

I used to give John money so he could buy cocaine. One day I bought a $50 purchase of coke and we made crack out of it. Then I took the pipe and pretended to get a hit out of it, and John was offended, and he wouldn't let me have any of the coke that I bought. He did the whole thing right in front of me. And I couldn't say share with me, because I was unable to stand up in front of him.

Soon John had done $600 worth of cocaine off me, not counting all the restaurants that we went to. One day we went to the Hilltop Steakhouse on rt. 1 in Saugus. And after the meal we went back to the car, and John said he was going to beat me up. So we were both in the car, with me at the wheel, and he said he was going to beat me up. So I said I "alright", and I grabbed the keys and bolted outside and ran back into the restaurant. I passed everyone in line and made my way to the dining room. I grabbed a waitress and said "can you call the police for me?", and she said there's a cop right cover there. So I got to the police officer and said "there's a black man and he's going to beat me up. For John was right behind me, and the cop said "calm down or I will beat you up too." So I told the cop what happened and he detained John. I had the option of leaving him there with the cop, but I figured if I left him there I would never see my $600. So I said he can come with me, and I convinced him not to beat me up.

But then John would take my car, and he kept it for days. He had his own car, but he always used mine. And when I was done working my shift at Toys R Us, he had the car and was over an hour late. I had to wait for this guy, and then he took my car when I was working at Hogan/Berry, he was over an hour late.

I wanted to go home and sleep, having just finished the night shift. Some time we would go over his friends house in Lynn, and I would sleep on the couch. The guy there had friends that used to do crack there, but I didn't smoke because I was a Christian, and I refused the crack, and witnessed for the Lord for these couple of guys.

One day me and John went to some guy's house, and John went in. I left him there playing a joke on him. From there on he always took the keys, from me. I couldn't leave him again. He said he was going to a friends house and he said 'these people are Christians'. "I was like" what am I? dog meat?" But I said nothing. So I had to sit in the car, in the cold for over an hour while he smoked crack. My feet got cold as I only had dress shoes on. Finally he came back, and got in and instead of bitching to him how cold I was, I played it light, and said thank god you're back, my feet are freezing. Instead of saying, "how dare you keep me in the cold for over an hour.".

Then John had a girlfriend stay over my house, and I went to work. The next morning John said "we did it over you're bureau, because I didn't want to disrespect your bed." But I believe he just said that, and did it in my bed. He said, I think she gave me something", meaning a std. And I was secretly glad.

Then the last deal with John was, he went to the bank and he was going to pay me back the $600. He went into the bank, and came out about 10 minutes later, and said they were closed. A lie. Because if you go through the doors before closing they let you do your banking before they close. He said they were closed and I didn't get my money.

Finally with John, we went to Stop and Shop and got a cash withdrawal of $50 from them. John wanted $200 for cocaine. So we went to three other area Stop and Shops and I got $50 from each store and gave him $200. He did the coke, and I got none. So John ripped me off over $800. And he was gone out of my life.

Chapter 44
The Nova and The Z Car

So I had a 1967 Chevy II Nova, black with a 350v8, and Cragar wheels. It never ran right after I blew the first engine up. It was always missing. I brought it over to Whitehead Motors on Poplar St. in Gloucester. While their someone broke into the car and stole my radio, and speakers from the back. I asked Whitehead to reimburse me for the radio and speakers, but he said he wasn't responsible. What a jerk! I like to call him Whitehead expert ripoffs. He couldn't get the car to run right anyways.

So I sold it to Bryan McTurn. He didn't make his payments that he was supposed to. So my uncle Dave hopped in it and repossed the car White McTurn, was in the little store. Dave brought the car back to my house on White's Mtn. Rd. and he hid it in the bottom of the little hill in the driveway. McTurn came up about 20 minutes later and pulled all his stuff in the car.

So a couple nights later I went out with McTurn, and Phil Haynes, and a couple of girls. We got stoned and then I was in the back seat by myself and McTurn got in the front. He started punching me in the face. He knocked me from one side of the seat to the other. He just kept hitting me and hitting me. Finally he said "look at me" so I looked thinking this was the end of it. But he punched me some more.

Finally the beating stopped, and they brought me home. They dropped me off at my house, and McTurn stepped out to pee, and there was a baseball bat there, and I was going to smash it over McTurn's head, but I decided not to do it. So I went home, and looked in the mirror. I was beaten black and blue everywhere on my face. I was going to call the cops, but that wouldn't have been cool, so I didn't.

My uncle Dave never got him back for that. I saw McTurn hitchhiking a couple days later on the highway. I picked him up and I don't know where this came from but I told him "I forgive you". It blew his mind. Then I dropped him off. I don't remember what happened to the Nova.

A couple months later I got the Datsun 240 Z car from my father in KY. It was red with a black hood, and a roll bar in the back. The thing was fast. I brought it up from KY., and on the way I had to stop every 10 miles and blow out the gas filter, because the tank had rust in it and the engine would stall. Then finally the lights gave out and I was driving in the dark. So I pulled off at the next exit, and I saw a police car, and I told the officer I had no lights. He then escorted me down the highway to the next exit, where he drove to a gas station. Luckily they had a mechanic on duty. But luckily again since this was a Rally Z car it had fog lamps mounted on the bumper. The mechanic ran a wire from the battery to the fog lights and hooked them up. And I was on my way again.

The Z car was cool. I drove it to work one day at the paint factory. This guy had a VW Scirroco, and he wanted to race me at the parking lot. I said sure and we started off. I easily beat him to the end of the driveway and was first going out the road.

A couple days later the Z car broke down and I parked it at the drive in theater, on Concord St. I left it there one day to long, because McTurn found out this was my car, and smashed out all my windows. He smashed out the front windshield, and the back, and the sides.

So I got my the front windshield replaced. And I drove it around with just the front window. One night me and my friend Jim Spiro, went to Boston in it. And I parked it on a side street. Me and Gump went carousing around. We went to a couple bars, looking to score some weed. After a crummy night, to top it all off, someone smashed my front window again. I started driving back, and somehow I made a wrong turn on a one way street. Instantly there was 5 cop cars there, and they boxed me in. And found a kind of knife which they confiscated. And they let me go saying "get this car out of Boston"! So I drove home with a spider web on my front window, going 80 miles an hour. The fragments of the windshield were swaying, and could have broke off and hit me in the eye. Luckily it held and I drove home.

So I got another front window to replace the broken one again. And the Z car needed welding done to its frame, because I had jumped it over a small hill in the road, and the frame wasn't holding up, so I drove it back to KY. Along the way, along the Pennsylvania/Maryland border it broke down. So I abandoned it and started hitchhiking. I got a ride from some guy in a delivery truck, and he brought me to Cumberland, MD. I got out and called my father. He said he would come and get the car, and towed it back to KY. So I hitchhiked back to PA, and the waiting Z car. The guy who picked me up was drinking beer, and he offered me one. I refused, and told him about the Lord. So I left a good example of a Christian to him. So at the car, I waited for my father. He showed up late that night and found the car just where I told him it was, under an overpass. He hooked the car to the trailor, with a friend of his, who does body work for my father's cars. And I slept in the back of the truck on a mattress they put in there. That was the end of the Z car.

Chapter 45

The Wabbit and The Pathfinder

So I got a new car from my father, a 1977 white VW Rabbit, with black pinstripes, and a sticker that said "WABBIT" on the front window. It was a good running car. I went to NH with my friend Jim Spiro, and on the way back I pulled over to get gas. I checked the engine oil level on the dipstick. It's a good thing I did because it needed 2 quarts of oil. So I drove it to work everyday, and parked it on the side of the parking lot. One day it popped out of gear, and rolled down to the truck loading zone. They called me out of work to move it. No biggy. So I traded the "WABBITT" that said I "JESUS SAVES" on the bumper for a brand new 1987 Nissan Pathfinder. It cost me $329/month. I had to put my own stereo system in it because it did not come with a sound system. I put a new stereo, and speakers on the sides of the back seats, and an equalizer. The thing could jam. So I also bought a little vacuum cleaner, that you plug in to the cigarette lighter, and would always vacuum it. I waxed it all the time, and kept the dashboard clean with Armorall. I also rotated the tires. One day at work I parked it next to the little parking space next to the paint dept. side of the plant, and the main boss Ralph said I had to move it and not park there anymore. No biggy.

One day they asked me to drive some paint cans to Bliss Marine in Woburn, they gave me gas money and extra money. I would have liked to do that all day if possible.

So one day I was driving on Washington St. in Gloucester towards the rotary, and I was thinking about Holly. And I made believe she was in the car with me. And I wasn't paying attention and I rammed the van in front of me. The Pathfinder was hit bad but still drivable. So I drove with a smashed up front end. And I quit work and my mother told me I can't afford it anymore, and to give it back to the dealer. So I stupidly listened to her advice and got rid of the SUV.

Chapter 46
The Cops and Fred

The school buses were all parked at the abandoned drive in theater. And Fred Armstrong, and I, and Bobby Monroe were breaking into the snack bar, and the busses. One day the cops came to Bobby Monroe's house to ask about the breakins. Me and Bobby were at my house when Bobby's mother called and said we have to come down to see the cops. We were both high as a kite, so we ducked our heads into my grandfather's pool on the way down to Bobby's house, to make it look like we were swimming to hide our red eyes. When we got to Monroe's house the cops were there and they were asking us questions. "Who broke into the snack bar"?", we said "Fred", "who broke into the busses?", we said "Fred", "who vandalized the premises?", and we held our tongues for a second; and the cop said "Fred?" and we both laughed and said "yes". So there really wasn't much punishment. We had to clear the yard and cut brush with grass cutters. I had to go back to PA, so I didn't do much work. I left it for Bobby, and Fred to do.

Chapter 47

Apartments

I lived with my friends, Bob Store, and Jim Spiro, at the "top of the harbor", in W. Gloucester. We lived there for a few months, and we took a fourth guy to stay in my room. Then me and Bob, and Craig Rune, and my cousin Jeff, lived on Sadler St. One day there was a breakin, at the apartment. And someone stole Craig's stereo, and speakers. But they didn't touch mine. He believed Bob Store did it and made it look like someone else did it. But he didn't touch mine because he knew I was a man of God.

Then I lived at 2 Riggs St. which was my sister's house. Me and Greg Myers were roommates. He was cool. Then he moved out and Craig Rune lived there. Then he moved out and Dave Gabby moved in with his 10 year old son. He was the roommate from hell. He was the worst roommate I ever had. He used to put his plates back on the shelf after having his dinner without washing them, saying "I am a clean eater." I said "I don't care how clean you are, there's a thing called germs"! And I got him to do his dishes.

Then he came home drunk one night, and I was in my room trying to sleep. He started bitching about all the milk being gone. And he came in my room, and backed me up to the corner on my bed. He was going to beat me up, and God gave me the fist to fight back, but then he stopped his attack. He was the worst roommate I ever had.

Chapter 48

Kevin Hanes

Then back at my apartment above the Action Shelter, my friend Kevin Haynes came over to sleep over. Then at night as I was lying on my bed, and he was on the couch, he said "do you want to come?" and I was thinking (what is he gonna call a couple girls?). But then he comes over to my bed, all baliky bare ass and goes "move over". So I put my arm up to block him and said "no fucking way, get the heck out of here!" So he went back to the couch, I couldn't sleep that night. He was the last person I thought would be homosexual.

Kevin was into the cocaine big time. I had another apartment that I lived in with Kevin, his girlfriend, (I guess he was bisexual because he had a girlfriend), and an old man. Kevin would borrow my car, and he and his girlfriend, would drive to Lynn, to get coke. I stayed behind and waited for them all the time. Then they would come home and do up all the coke. I could of had some but I wanted to be an example of a Christian, and I didn't want to smoke any crack.

One time Kevin robbed the White Hen Pantry with a knife. He wanted me to drive the getaway car. I was like (no way am I driving the getaway car). He got caught and spent 5 years in Middleton jail. Then he got out and robbed the store again and got caught and spent another 5 years in jail. What a waste product.

Chapter 49
The Heights A Cape Ann

Then I had an apartment at the Heights at Cape Ann. It was cool because they had a exercise room. Every night I would go on the machines and watch the Red Sox. I bought a computer and my cousin Jeff helped me set it up.

I had a friend stay there for a while. He was from Bulgaria, and every morning like clockwork, I would drive him to his job downtown. He had the good life, a place to stay, steady work. But he wanted to cheat. He stole two checks from me for $400, and cashed them. The bank got his picture on the camera at the window. And I identified him and told the bank he stole the checks. The bank wanted to press charges right away. But I gave him a couple days to pay back, giving him a grace period. But he failed to repay so I got the bank to come after him. He went to court and the judge deported him back to Bulgaria. I called him the Bulgarian motherfucker.

One day at the heights I decided to walk to town down the train tracks, behind the apartment complex. It was a snowy day and much snow on the ground. I got to the bridge tunnel, and the train was coming. I had to get off the tracks, quickly. So was undecided as to which way to get off. (do I go left or do I go right.?). And I went right. Bad mistake because I was sucked up against the wall with the train bearing down on me. There was like a foot and a half of space between me and the train. And I was standing on snow. If I had slipped I would have had my legs amputated from me, because I would have fallen under the wheels. So luckily the train went by and I walked towards town.

Then at the apartment I had b.o. (body odor). My whole apartment was a disgusting stench. The smell was so strong that it went through the door and out the hallway. I don't know how it got to smell so bad. But the management came by and wrote a note on my door saying to take the trash out, because that's what they thought the odor was from. I moved out a couple days later.

Chapter 50

The Fire

While living at my mother's house I had friends I drank with. Carl Hermdorf, and Steve Johnson. They were hardcore drinkers. They always drank Natural Ice because it was cheap. I'm like if you are gonna drink beer, get something that tastes good. That's why I always drank Samuel Adams, and Stella Artois. But Carl and Steve had the DT's., and they would drink past the DT's. And start shaking. Then they would drink back to the DT's. Instead of stop drinking to get below the DT's, and stop shaking. They kept on drinking past the DT's. They had it rough.

But one day I was on the phone with them, and after I hung up I was undecided to go to their house in W. Gloucester or not. And I was like (should I stay here or go there? Should I stay here or go there?") So I decided to stay home. It turned out to be a fatal mistake. That night Steve and Carl tried to light a fire in the basement. The house was all wood. All wooden floors, walls, and ceilings, not to the kitchen walls, and roof. So they were trying to light a fire but it wouldn't catch. So they kept throwing capfuls of acetone on it. Capful after capful, and suddenly it caught fire. And the flames came shooting out of the fireplace and taught the couch on fire. Soon the couch was aflame, and it spread to the wooden walls. Soon the whole basement was on fire. And the flames quickly spread to the first floor, and it was on fire. But the tragedy of that night was there was a girl

114

sleeping in the upstairs, and the fire soon filled the upstairs and it caught fire. And the girl was screaming but she perished in the flames that night. The whole house burned to the ground. If I had been there I might have been able to save her. And I was sorry I didn't go there that night.

Chapter 51
Uncle Saul

So I stayed one summer at my uncle Saul's and aunt Loretta's house in Middleton, RI. In 1985 or so. And I had to tear down an old wooden barn. It was the size of an ordinary house, and I tore that barn down piece by piece, from the slate roof to the dirt floor. I filled like 5 dumpster rolloffs. And I made money for him by selling the 3x10's that I took down. I put them in a separate pile, and sold them to interested parties. There were two barns there, side by side and the one I tore down became the driveway for the second barn, which he made into an apartment house.

My cousin Shane and PJ, Saul's sons used to play football in the side yard. Shane played midget football for the Middleton Islanders. We used to go to his games every week. He played linebacker. He was so good he played for the US Naval Academy. He starred as a linebacker for the Navy, at the Army/Navy game in Philadelphia. Saul videotaped the game which was on national television.

While working at Saul's house I had lunch everyday for 1 hour. Saul thought this was a little too long. I used to go to the little convenience stores down the street and buy the Boston Herald. Lorretta was always watching the 700 club at lunch. Then I bought Axis and Allies at the toy store, and Conquest of the Empire. Two excellent games, and we played everyday.

I went out gillnetting with Saul one night, me and this other guy. We were working on the nets when Saul caught a dolphin in the net. I wanted to see it but I didn't see it because I was too busy with the nets with the other guy. We went to sleep that night in the bow and the guy said "this is better then sex". The next day we went to shore with our catch. Saul gave me the opportunity to go out with him again, but I declined. I watched the super bowl at his father's house. The cowboys won. And that was the end of Saul.

Chapter 52
Paul

Then I had a friend named Paul Silver. He lived on Cedarwood St. in W. Glouc. He lived in a house that was a pig sty. The dishes were piled up in the sink, the walls were kicked out, and there were junk stereo receivers all over the place, because his father worked at Panasonic. All the kids used to hang out at his house.

Paul was an unsuccessful entrepreneur. He tried to sell Mother's brand waxes, and washes for cars. But that didn't work and he got stuck with a lot of product. He tried to harvest seaweed to fish companies, but that failed. He tried to do paintball business, when he bought a lot of paintball guns, and ammo, and he would rent out the guns, to the kids to have fun in the woods. But that failed. He had a digital cafe., on Pleasant St. where he had a whole store of computers that all the kids would play after school. But that failed.

Paul had a crush on my sister, Cathy. But finally she didn't want him anymore. So he stood by the door of her room, to cry to her. But I strong armed him out of there. Then he ran off into the pit road and went to the top of the pit. A sheer cliff about 100ft. high. He was going to jump off. But I caught up to him, and said "Paul, you don't want to do that." And I convinced him not to jump.

Me, and Paul, and my cousin Jeff, built a deck for my mother's house. It came out pretty good, and he paid me pretty well. That was the end of Paul.

Chapter 53
Mount Washington

Me, and my friend Danny, Jim, my brother, I think, my sister, I think, and my mother, climbed up Mt. Washington, in NH. We climbed it in like 2 hours. There was one part of the mountain that left the trail. And I figured I could cut some time of the hike by climbing this slope in front of me. But by the time I had finished climbing this slope, the rest of my party had caught up to me following the regular trail. So we made it to the top and looked around. We were so tired, we walked back down the auto road. Then we flagged down this guy in a truck, and we all piled into the back bed of the truck. The guy drove us down the mtn., and he dropped us off at my Pathfinder, we never would have made it without that ride.

Chapter 54

Mount Katadin

Then me and my friend Danny, and Jim, and my mother climbed Mt. Katadin in ME. That was a very difficult climb. You had to use metal rods to pull yourself up that were pounded into the rocks. Along the way I met this man coming down the mountain, and I told him I was a smoker, and I needed refreshment. He gave me dried fruit and water, which I was thankful for. So me and Danny made it to the top, but there was an extension of rocks piled high that went out to the side an extra 1/8 of a mile. Danny walked it out and back, but I didn't go, I just watched him climbing. Then we all made it back to base camp, at different speeds. Danny came in first along with my mother who had turned around mid climb. Then I came in next, then Jim. That was the end of Mt. Katadin.

Chapter 55

Eastern River Expeditions

Then me and Danny, my mother, my sister, and who else Paul went on the Eastern River Expedition. It was a white water rafting trip on the Eastern river, in Maine. You put your car in the parking lot, and you get on a bus that takes you to the head waters of the Eastern river. Its about a 20 minute bus ride. Then you get off and you get into a huge inflatable raft. There was about 8 rafts and 9 people/raft. The guide sits in back, along with Paul and Cathy, my sister. My mother and her friend in the middle, two other ladies on the trip with us in the middle too, and me and Danny my friend up front.

Then they open the flood gates at the head waters and all the dammed up water came gushing out, and it propelled your raft down the river, about category 4 white water rapids. The guide yells to us "all forward", which meant, you dip your paddle in the water and pulled the oar. Me and Danny in front high fived our paddles in the air clicking them together. At one point the water got steady and we slowed down a bit. There was another raft on the side of the river, stopped and resting. I yelled out "All forward"! Our guide got a little nervous when I said that.

Then our guide asked us if anyone wanted to get towed behind our raft, and I said "I do". The guide gave me a rope that was attached to the back of the raft, and I was pulled along in the water, behind the raft. The guide told me to keep my feet in front of me, just in case there were any rocks in the way. That was fun being towed along behind the raft.

At one point of the journey there was a place where they made a video of you going down the water. You could buy the video back at base camp for like $20. Finally at the end of river expedition they gave you a bbq feast. There was a little lake there and I was contemplating walking on the water. Paul was there and he thought I was going to do it. But then I realized if I walked on the water there would be a media buzz and I did not want that, so I didn't walk on the water.

Back at base camp they showed you your video of the little part of the river that you went down. We saw our trip but didn't buy it. And that was the end of the ERE.

Chapter 56
The Suzuki RM 125

I had a 1988 Suzuki RM 125, big and tall in the saddle, a real nice bike which I paid $1000 for. I got the kid I bought it from to throw in a pair of riding boots for $100 he was asking for, as part of the deal.

So I had the 125 for about a year and I wanted to sell it. So I took out an ad in the paper, and was asking $500 for it. So this guy calls me up and says "I'm taking it today". Which sounded kind of funny to me. I just thought he was sure intending in buying the bike today. So the guy comes over to my sister's barn were I had the bike, and he says "I couldn't find your house, so I left my truck at the bottom of the hill, and I walked up here." I thought that was a little strange, but I believed the guy. So the guy gets on the bike and I told him just go down to the church, do a couple donuts and come back. So the guy says 'OK' and he left with the bike. So about 5 minutes or so goes by and I don't hear him. I thought maybe he's on the side of the road bleeding somewhere. So I walked down the hill and came to the neighbors which were outside and I asked them if they saw a guy on a motorcycle, they said "no." So the freaking crook must have come down the hill, and threw the bike into the back of his truck and took off. I called the cops, they came and took information and from me about the bike.

The brazen thief had the balls to come back the next day, and stole two of Caleb's mmtn. Bike. Caleb is my sister's ex husband. I never recovered financially from that hit. What a prick he was.

Chapter 57
Caleb

I have had many entanglements with Caleb. First Caleb is a mountain biker. He started his own line of bikes called Sinister Bikes. He had two partners from northern New England. Frank the welder, and Sky Nacel. Caleb built an elaborate obstacle course for mountain bikes. He built a bridge, a couple of jumps, and the ferocious teetor totter. You go up on this thing and when in the middle you go down the board and down a 25' rock almost straight down. You have to be suicidal to go down this thing. Caleb built other bridges and obstacles in the woods behind my sister's house. Then he built a pump track. Its just a small oval shaped course where there is three ooped de doos, and a berm on each end. Its 1/16 mile long so 16 times around is a mile. I only went a couple laps on the thing. The course was built on the side of the driveway. So I wrote a story about Caleb, and his mountain bike adventures. It is started out "In the Wild Woods of W. Gloucester, a man has turned his love for mountain bikes into a business, a hobby, and a pastime. It was about 5 pages long.

Caleb and I have had many battles, both verbal and physical. We would argue religion. Caleb is a body builder, and he is much stronger than I. He gets stressed out very easily. We were at my grandmother's house and Caleb wasn't there more than 5 minutes and he goes "I'm stressed". What a burnout. So one day Caleb and I fought. He pushed me into the cabinet and I just took him and threw him down on the floor. He then yells out "Cathy your brother John is out of control". What a wimp. So another day me and Caleb wrestled in a fight in the house. He got me down and I went in the guard position, like they do in the UFC. He let me get up and we went out on the outside deck for round two. If this had been a fist fight I would have won. But this turned into another wrestling match, and he got me down and pinned. Then he says "You've had karate training, I haven't. Then I got up.

Another time I went to his house at night to look for something I had lost. I couldn't find it so I left a note for Caleb to look for it. I didn't know he was in the bedroom with his girlfriend. So he comes out and strong arm's me outside on the deck. He pulled me along by the arm and I said "come on Caleb". But he pulled me outside and said "I will fucking kill you!" He pulled his arm back to swing but didn't punch. So he was pushing me against the door, and he said "I will throw you off this porch"! and I said "you will go to jail"! Then we threw each other down the steps. They were wooden steps, and we went down all the way. Then I looked at him and said "fuck you"!, and I left. I had to go to the doctor's office for like a pinched nerve in my neck. And that was the end of Caleb.

Chapter 58
The Fire Works

One night me and the gang, Bobby Monroe, John Rambert, Paul Temple, Fred Armstrong, Karate Man Dave, Brad Williamson, Phil Haynes, shot fireworks off at each other. We split into two armies at the Cape Ann Bible Church parking lot at each end. And we had plastic sleds to use as a shield from the incoming bottle rocket attack. I had a plastic sled to use as a shield, good thing too, because I had to block a few bottle rockets headed my way. We had 8ball Roman candles too. And we shot back and forth at each other. When we were done it was like a war zone, with smoke everywhere. It was cool.

Chapter 59

The Jumping Jehovas

That same night me and the aforementioned gang threw snowballs at the Jehova Witness "church" door, we kept pelting and pelting away at the door with continuous snow balls. Then all of a sudden the door burst open and about 10 jumping Jehovas come running out. We split up in like 5 different directions, they could never find us. Soon they all went back inside, and we just laughed. That was fun.

Chapter 60
The Fire

I went to my uncles garage one night, and it was cold out. He had a little propane heater going with an open flame providing heat. I stood there with my back to the flame warming myself. Soon I realized that I was standing too close for too long because my pants caught fire, in the pocket. Then I started yelling 'I'm on fire. I'm on fire'. So my uncle Dave tried to put me out with his gloved hand. Soon the flames were extinguished and I was not on fire anymore. I felt all right at first then about a half hour later it hurt like hell. So I went to the hospital and they gave me morphine. Then my uncle came to pick me up because they said I couldn't drive. But my uncle said "you'll be alright, fuck them". So I drove home. I had to have a dressing of clothe bandages held on by tape. I had to go to the doctors' office everyday for a week to change the bandages. One night my friend "Barn Kelly" changed my dressing at my sister's house. So my drawers were dropped and 'Barn Kelly' changed the dressing. Just then my sister showed up with her boyfriend Tony, and my ass was exposed and they saw Cathy changing my bandage and they started laughing. I said this ain't funny and they apologized.

Soon the burn mark in my leg went away along with the pain, and I was fine but I learned my lesson around that propane heater.

Chapter 61
The Horses

One night as I lay in bed the horses got out and they ran all the way down Black's Mtn. Rd. to the highway route 128. Where they got hit by cars and died. My brother actually ran over the head of one of the horses, I later learned. Then he came back to my room and said it was all my fault they got out, which it wasn't, and he wanted to fight me. I said I don't fight because its against my religion and he left. But I realized my brother could kick my ass. Well there was no way I was going to let that happen that my brother could beat me, so I took up karate to learn to fight. I loved it. I went to Tom Wilson's Health and Self Defense class. I went through the belts quickly. About half way through my belts Tom headed for San Francisco with his daughter to take up psychiatry. So his protoge Matt Brun took over the class with half of the floor space as Tom rented it out to what is now the Barking Lot. I made it to 1st degree green belt with Matt. It was fun learning katas and pinions. Then Matt stopped the class and that was the end of that.

Chapter 62

Matt

I ended up moving Matt like 5 times. We put all his furniture in the back of my truck and I moved him from house to house. One time we went to Rhode Island to get his girlfriend and her stuff. We picked her up and her stuff and they fought in the truck. We ended up going to a Chinese restaurant. Later Matt took her home to his house and about a week later he came home and she lay dead on the bed. She died from too much alcohol in her system. It was very saddening for Matt. And I felt bad for him. I told Matt this is a wake up call for you because she died in her sins, and was lost eternally in hell. I said this is your time to decide for Christ. Weather he did or not I don't know.

But Matt is a funny guy, he was working at Flannagan's gas station. He said he was a petroleum dispenture technision. Or something like that. Then he got a job driving cab. I am still friends with Matt today.

Chapter 63
The Ring

I had a high school class ring that I was very fond of. It was silver with white crystal birth stone. And it said "JOHN" on one side and "1984" on the other. Then on one side it had a symbol of the voc school carpentry class emblem, and on the other side it had a picture of the devil. And it said RUSSELL HIGH SCHOOL on the top next to the birth stone, on the inside was my name John Banner in cursive on the inside.

So one day I was working at my little old lady friend's house Arlene. And I lost my ring somewhere in the yard. I looked high and low but I did not find it. So I was all bummed out because I wore this ring on my finger for 30 years. I purposely bought the ring two sizes too big for my finger so that I would fit me later in life. And it fit good.

But Arlene's nephew went walking around the yard and he went home to NH. But there on the tread of his boot my ring was lodged in the tread of his boot. And he called me and said I have it and I said its mine. And he says "can you prove it?" And I said "yeah it says "John" on one side and "1984" on the other". And he says "can you further prove it?" And I said "yeah it says John Banner on the inside". And he said "I guess its yours". So he mailed it to Arlene's house. It took a week to get it from NH and Arlene said "If God wants you to have this ring the post office is not going to stop it." So the box finally came in the mail and I tore it open and there was my ring. That was a true miracle from God.

Chapter 64

Bobby Mercury

I met Bobby Mercury at the Webber II Unit in Addison Gilbert Hospital. The nurses called us the John and Bob show, because we used top feed of each others energy. We were great friends in there. We used to sing Led Zepplin's "Whole Lot of Love" to each other with air guitars.

So time went on and we moved on not seeing each other for a while. Then I saw him in Beverly on Cabot St. I pulled over and talked to him. He said something about drinking beer and I was being a Christian and not liking it. So I left him there.

A few years later we hooked up again. He used to come to my apartment on Fort Square, and wake me up. He always made me depressed when he came over because he would talk to himself and sing Beatles songs. I was regretfully starting to drink again at that time. And one night we went out drinking in my Ford F150. We bought a couple six packs and he had a couple nips. We went down to the Wingaersheek beach parking lot and pulled over. He drank beer after beer after beer. At that time he was a full blown alcoholic. So we left there and I dropped him off at the Hillcrest House where he was staying. But the only thing was Bobby was passed out in the truck. So I got to the house and alerted the staff about Bobby. I thought they would take him and throw him in bed. But instead they called the police and the paramedics. So the EMT's came and they gave him narcane to arouse him. The police searched my truck and said I was not in trouble, thank God, and they took Bobby away in the ambulance to the hospital. I had to have my truck and they towed it away to Blackburn Circle. It cost me $185 that night to get it out of custody. Thanks Bobby.

Chapter 65
The Apartment

So I rented an apartment it on Fort Square or "the Fort". It was a third floor apartment with bedroom, bathroom, kitchen, and living room. The day the landlord showed me this place I saw the view, and I said immediately "I'll take it." The view was so fantastic. You could see the St. Peter's marina, the legion, the Blackburn tavern, the Chinese restaurant, and the coffee shop, the Cape Ann Savings bank, the whale watch boats, "the Yankee Freedom" and "the Privateer IV", the schooner "the Thomas Landon", the building center, and the Gloucester house".

The first day I moved in there, I had the church friends help me move. And someone put a box on the stove and accidently turned the burner on and it started fire, on the stove. The firemen had to come and put it out. Not a great way to make friends with the neighbors, and landlord, starting a fire on the first day I moved in there. So I went to ask the church people "which one of you did it?" And no one stepped up to take responsibility. Oh well.

So I had a cat named O.J. with me. He was so cool. He was all orange, so I called home O.J. after orange juice. He used to come up with me on the couch and sit, and gnaw on my hand, it didn't hurt but his scratches hurt. He used to sleep with me. I would go to bed and call his name, and he would come to bed with me. I used to put him under the covers, and block every exit with the blankets, but he always found a way to escape. Then I would sleep on my left side and he would be there. Then I rolled to my right side, and he would come over to my right side. He used to like hiding in the shower stall. And he would visit me when I was on the pot.

So I had around 3 or 4 different people living in the next door apartment across the hall. And a woman named Teri moved in next door. And when my door was open to visit Teri, her door would be open and O.J. would go over to Teri's apartment. He used to come in and say "hi". He could talk, and sing for his supper. He used to investigate Teri's apartment and look for mice. He used to go in her bedroom and wouldn't come out. Sometimes I just left him in there and Teri would throw him over to my side when he came around. He used to have matted hair, and I pulled his fur, but it hurt him, so I left him with the matts. One night Teri said O.J. was our child. I thought was cool, but I didn't say anything.

Chapter 66
Emily

Then my cousin Emily moved in for a while. She had two dogs, and a mccaw, bird of paradise. The only problem was the bird used to crow every morning around 5 am. and wake the neighbors, who could hear through the thin walls of the bedroom. So they got mad, and the landlord found out she was staying there, and he told me to get her out of my apartment. So I told her and she moved out.

Chapter 67
Bobby Mercury Again

So then my friend Bobby Mercury used to come over to my apartment and wake me up. I always got depressed when he came by because he would talk to himself and sing Beatles songs. When I finally got up in the morning I used to drink beer with Bobby in the apartment. He made me mad because he would always start a new beer even though he wasn't finished with this current beer in hand. Then he made messes with his cigarette butts, and he left food out. He threw bacon on the floor, and knocked over my boom box to the floor. So I took him and threw him on the floor of the kitchen. And he was lying there and I didn't care and I went to hit him again, but laid off.

One night Bobby came over and he got drunk. He was leaving the apartment and down the stairs, when he fell head long down the stairs and passed out. His head was blocking the door at the bottom of the steps. So the neighbor called 911 and the police came, and the paramedics came over. Finally Bobby came around and said to the paramedics "I'm John Lennon!" The EMT's were like a "OK".

So Bobby went to the hospital that night and the landlord found out and he said Bobby can't come over anymore. So I told Bobby not to come over any more. But he came over one time, and I said don't raise your voice, and don't sing Beatles songs, because he used to raise his voice. But that was it for Bobby, and I said don't come over anymore.

Chapter 68

Martha

I worked for Martha a couple times on various moving jobs. Martha was a hoarder, she never threw any trash away.

One night it was freezing out, and Martha was outside in the cold, overburdened with many suitcases and bags. So I did the Christian thing to do, and I took her in. She stayed with me about a month for one stint, and a second stint about a month. It was a cool relationship like husband and wife without the sex. But she turned my house into a storage unit. The landlord found out she was staying there and told me to get her out of there.

So I told her she had to go, and I left the house. When I got back Martha was still there talking on the phone. And I said "Martha you have to go. What are still doing here?" So I packed her up with all her junk in my bedroom, and about 3 hours late, I had Martha all moved out. But she left behind a table, an a/c unit, and 4 or 5 bags and suitcases.

One day she wanted me to go to the court with her. I went to a couple meetings of hers with her lawyer. So we went to the court and went through security. She placed her bag on the conveyor belt, and when it went through there showed up a knife on screen.

So she had to dump her bag on the table, and all the trash came out. Just trash, and trash, and more trash. I was embarrassed, I don't know how Martha felt, probably nothing at all. So finally they found the knife and she placed all her junk back in the bag. We went upstairs to the court and she had trial. The judge found her mentally ill and she was put in handcuffs and ankle shackles. I waited for her after court and got to talk to her in the little viewing room surrounded by glass with a little peep hole to talk through. I took her final instructions and they took her away. She had to go to Worcester State hospital for like two months or so.

But she still had her junk at my house, and I left message after message on her answering machine that my house is not a storage unit. So it took months to get all her stuff out. I brought bags out little by little. I only met Martha a couple time after that at the food pantry. And that was the end of Martha.

Chapter 69

The Suicide Attempt

So I was drinking a lot there at the apartment. I was a weekend warrior drinking 3 beers/night on Fridays and Saturdays, and a 6 pack on Sundays. After church watching football. But I could drink the whole 6 pack and not even get a buzz. So I was wasting alot of money and I decided to quit. But my mental illness was too much for me and I decided to take my life.

So I lay in bed with a knife one night, and I started to slit my wrist. I started hacking away with a knife but it wasn't cutting good so I got a different knife. And stupid me, I never tried to kill myself before, so I didn't know that once you cut your wrist the blood would come streaming out. But once I cut myself it was just a trickle of blood. I have a scar on my wrist to this day. So I didn't die that night, but the next day I still wanted death. So I took my Clozaril pills, and I swallowed a hand full of pills. I had them in like a gum ball of the medicine, and I was popping them in and out of my mouth. So finally I swallowed the Clozaril and I took the rest of my prescription, about half a bottle full and I took them too. So all this medicine was inside me, and I told Teri what I did and told her to take care of O.J. But my mother was outside in her car, and she called the EMT's. But before they arrived I got in the car with my mother she rushed me to the hospital.

So I went in the ER room and told them I swallowed a bunch of Clozaril. And they gave me charcoal to eat. And that produced a vomit of the pills. So I was lying in the little room with a security guard right outside, so I could not run away. As I lay there a handful of people came in to see me. One guy started to talk about his fishing trip. I hope the next time he tries to commit suicide someone won't talk about their fishing trip on him.

So as I was laying there, my mother invited her two sisters to see me. I looked and there were my two aunts at the door. Believe me that was the last thing I wanted to see. My mother apologized for that. So I spent the night at Addison Gilbert Hospital and they watched me sleep all night long. The next morning they brought me to Bayridge Hospital in Lynn. "Lynn, Lynn, the city of sin, you never come out the way you went in."

Chapter 70
My Experience at Bay Ridge

When I first got to Bay Ridge they scan you with a wand for security. Then you sit in like a side room waiting. Rather than sit and listen to the voices from the television I got up and had a sandwich. Then they bring you to Bayridge 1. They bring you to the quiet room and take all your clothes off except for your underwear.

Then they bring you to your room. They gave me a loud mouth, cursing roommate. I saw the chaplain and the roommate went by cursing, and I said to the chaplain "That's my roommate". Actually the roommate wasn't a bad guy once you get to know him. So there we were the two of us planning our lives.

We were in that room and suddenly I realized two weeks had gone by. I told him I was a Christian and suddenly we were buddies. He pushed his bureau over to mine. Then one day he pushed it back to his side. I said this is our sanctuary, where we can be alone with our thoughts. And it was.

I was standing by my bureau, thinking one day. And I stood in front of his bureau, but I caught myself, and said to myself "what are you doing?" I quickly stood in front of my bureau. Then I used to watch out the window at the outside paddock area, if you will. I was at the window tapping my hand on the window sill and my roommate came in and said "Freeze"! I froze, but then carried on because I had to.

One day I was on the toilet and they came in to the door and passed me my meds, while I was seated on the toilet. My roommate was there and he couldn't believe it. So I got off the commode and took my meds. Little did I know this was going to be a huge problem. I stepped on an ant in the bathroom while I was on the hopper, and I regretted it. But it became a battle for them to see my turds in the bowl as I kept flushing it before they could see. And I wanted them to see the turds, but I kept flushing it. So one day I took a crap in the trash bucket. And I had a note from God saying "Correction"! So I pulled the tirds out with a handful of toilet paper and flushed it, making the trash bucket clean again.

So the house cleaner was Hispanic, and it was time for me to change clothes, and the lady housekeeper came in at inappropriate times while I was getting changed. So I tried to speak Spanish to her in the hallway, but she wouldn't speak up. So one day they nabbed me and brought me into the quiet room and pulled my pants down and shot me with a needle of some shit, in both of my buttcheeks. They pulled my underwear down and I started yelling. The said "we haven't even injected you yet!" But I knew my butt was exposed and I yelled. The needle hurt and I yelled. One night while I was sleeping in my room they came in in the middle of the night and took my belt. I couldn't keep my pants up. I was walking around all over the place with one hand trying to keep my pants up for like a month.

Later after I got injected I pulled the bandages off my bum. One day I went to the milieu and sat down to eat. It seemed like everyone was staring at me from behind. I felt all the eyes on me. So when I got up I accidently knocked my chair over behind me. I stood up. So I made a statement with the chair. I told my roommate what happened and we both got a big kick out of it.

I my room I always stood in the doorway. And I looked at the guy who was running group meetings. I always looked at him and he at me but I never went to his group meetings till 2 months after.

I didn't know how much trouble I was in. A lawyer came to see me who represented a judge. This judge who I never saw committed me to 6 months in the hospital. I thought I would get out soon. So I was in bed one day and this lawyer came in who's name was Bill. So I called him sir, and started to get up. He said just stay in bed. And this judge who I never met sentenced me to six months.

So I played battleship with this guy one night. And we were engaged in battle and one of the staff came over and said this is "intense", and we finished the game. I won, but that was the last time I saw of that guy.

Chapter 71
The Food

The food was brought up every noon and every evening by black workers who brought the food up in a buffet style serving cart. The food was so disgusting you wouldn't feed it to your dog. And I had a baseball cap with the words "I am not ashamed, JESUS IS LORD." on it. It became difficult to speak because my hat said "I" for me and it was hard to say sentences starting with "I" because of the hat. And the black workers who brought the food up said "I like that hat." I felt good. But we all sat at dinner one night, and there was like 4 or 5 people around me and this guy said "whoa shit, I almost ate shit"! and I said "SALAD" as I was eating salad. And these were the first words I spoke in a long time.

Chapter 72
Bay Ridge Continued

So the cast of characters who came through that unit were different everyday. And every new guy was more psycho than the last. Everybody had a story about their mother. One guy I knew was a Christian, as he had adult visitors who talked to him about the Lord. One kid came in there with a bible. I let him go, but then decided to talk to him. I said "hey kid" "what version of the bible do you have there?" And he said "NIV". I said "ok". And we started to read it together. But he's all "I think its providence that we met each other here." And we wanted to have a church service. So we took little tubs of grape jelly, and mushed it with water, and stirred it til it became juice. Then we took a little cracker for bread. And we had a little church service in the tv room uninterrupted, with about 4 of us. He preached about how great this day was, seeing the birds outside the window. He preached on the armour of God, and this guy across from me knew the armour and he demonstrated the armour with his hands. So we had communion with the jelly that was made juice, and the crackers and I partook of it and a girl did too, that was cool. I had my bible with me too. It was NASB, but it was colored with crayon in some of the verses in Matthew. This was my bible that was given to me by my stepmother. I don't know how I got a hold of it, but the crayon scriptures were done by me at my father's trailor in KY, in 1983. I wasn't a Christian yet, but somehow I had underlined all these key scriptures in Matthew, and Romans, and the Corinthians, and the words were life to me as they magically ministered to me.

But like I say the cast of characters that came through there each day was more psychotic than the last. One guy came through there with long black hair, and he had a gown on. Everyone had a story to tell about their mother. This guy said his mother tried to kill him, or he tried to kill his mother, I forget which. But this guy was a definite psycho. He drank lots of coffee.

One guy was a Christian or not a Christian yet. He had a group of people to see him and they prayed for him. One day the kid was being prayed for in the back room I could tell because they were lifting their hands, and praying. So the psycho guy was just about to go in the room unawares. But I did the Lord's work by stopping him from going in.

Then there were big guys coming in there. And the inmates ran the show. Really the staff had problems with some people there. There were guys in particular that was scary. Two of them had "sin city" sweatshirts on. And they, made a drug deal in the milieu. I was scared to death. One guy wanted to kill me or beat me badly. Then there were two guys really big, one Hispanic, one black. The Hispanic guy had a tear drop tattoo below his eye, that means he killed someone. The other black guy was so big he couldn't fit under the shower head. He did jigsaw puzzles.

There were girls there too, some had tattoos. A group of them played Parcheise, and asked me to play. Parchiese to me is like rocket science, I had no idea how to play. But I just went along for the ride doing whatever they told me to do.

Every day I wore my JESUS hat. The black guys who brought in the "food", up every day said they liked my hat. But this big guy, the one in the "sin city" sweatshirt wanted to kill me. He said "what's up with the JESUS hat"? I disn't answer him yet. That night they showed a horror film in the milleau. I was scared to death. The horror movie in front of me, the guy who wanted to kill me behind me visiting his mother, in the backroom. So I had to confront this guy after his mother left. I told him "He is risen"!

We went into the back room and he started out by saying "have you ever been to a strip joint?" sadly I had to say yes. And then he said "have you ever done acid?" sadly I said yes. So I told him a little about the Lord.

And he said "I have faith". I said that's good. But still he wanted to kill me, so I ducked into my room which was right off the room we were in, and I closed the door. The guy started roaming around the room and I watched him from the window on my door, scared to death he was gonna come in and get me. But then he stopped right at my door, and a minute later, he was crying to one of the staff about his sobriety. I lucked out. He left a couple lays later.

One day this guy said to me while I was eating "are you a child molester?" I said no. He said "are you a rapist?" I said no. I thought (who the fuck is this guy asking me questions like that)? He left a day later.

Then they switched me to a different room, the one off the back room. The only way I can describe to the reader is that I was the Frankenstein monster trying to be nice, one day I met a guy from Gloucester, Tom. He was so funny, he did bird impressions by flapping his arms, like wings. I saw him somewhere from Gloucester, but can't remember where. We became fast friends.

We used to walk "fresh air" the fenced in walking area. We walked around and around the little complex. All the patients used to stand in the gazebo and watch a couple Gloucester guys walking and talking. I told him my theory about the meds. How that you take the meds into your stomach, how do they then go to your head? Eventually I learned they dissolve and go into your blood stream, and into your head.

One day me and Tom noticed a girl reading a book, and found out her name was Eva. She was from a small eastern block European nation. We found out she was in here because she drank too much cough syrup, almost a whole bottle and the judge sentenced her to Bay Ridge. She was reading a book about how the Nazis treated the Jews in WW II.

So I was like that's kinda the same thing that happened to me, but said nothing. So like I say I was the Frankenstein monster trying to be nice. I realized I was this monster and I noticed that day by day, Eva was sitting closer to where I was sitting. She was trying to get near to me. So I said to her "hi." But I knew its the monster, and I started to cry. She said "you don't have to cry." And we became friends.

One day this lady came in who was very much a busy body. She wanted to get in the face of the staff and patients. She was always confronting the staff with bullshit questions, like "what's your last name?" or "what's your first name?" to the staff. Everybody laughed at her as her situation became like a soap opera. She would be on telephone with her husband, and we all felt for that poor guy. Eventually he came to see her, and their daughter who was paralysed in a wheel chair. They talked in the back room, while the daughter talked in the milliue with her friend who came along. She had purple hair and was overweight. So as everybody was laughing at her dilemma, she brought the husband out of the room and marched down the hall. She said pretend its our wedding ceremony and she sang "here comes the bride" down the hall. Eventually in a different occasion she said she didn't feel safe in the unit. She talked to me and wanted to know my name. But the staff intervened and said "you don't have to know". The staff looked at me and I said I know the person I am and I have to be careful around her. The staff knew everything about me. More on that later.

So the one day the strange lady was acting up. Getting into the faces of everybody including the cleaning personal. And they put all of us into the hallway by the nurses station and locked the door for security. So I grabbed Eva and said "what's going on?", and Eva said "they put handcuffs on her and took her to Bay Ridge II.

Later I knew Eva was watching Disney cartoons outside my room in the little break room. I knew it was Eva even without seeing her. She was laughing at the cartoons.

But the staff knew my situation. The guy John said "I can read your mind". And I knew he could. I told him my theory of Noah's three sons. How each son went to a different part of the world, and started the races. One brother went to Asia, one went to Africa, and one went to Europe. We got into playing chess. And I always had to do what John said. If he said "sit here." I had to sit there. I had to do everything he told me. He even said to me "you're not a football player you're bench warmer". Because somehow he knew without me telling him how I went to a patriots game and I was on camera. But I was smoking a joint right when the camara was on me, and I didn't see myself on the big screen because of the joint. That's why he said I was a bench warmer. The woman who was there talked to me and wanted to know my situation. She knew the answers before I said them. She asked me "what's your favorite color?" she knew I liked green, even before I said it. Then she asked "what's your favorite group?" and she knew it was Boston without me saying it. And I didn't say Boston but I said "you know who!" to her.

One girl was there as long as I was. Each day she would figure me out a little more. She couldn't play scrabble very easily. I eventually told her that I love her.

The main girls would always sing "country roads" by John Denver. Everytime they sang that song I would get depressed. The one girl made a snake on paper colored it, and cut it out, like a real snake I looked at it and said "that's impossible". It was cut out of paper so precisely. I told her that Adam named all the animals. She was impressed.

Then the staff brought a girl through the quiet room. She was checked out by two men. I saw them bring her in there down the hall. When she got out she was noticeably shaken. The two guys probably stripped searched her. She wanted to take a shower to calm down. That was pretty low for the staff to do that.

One day a young kid in his early twenties was there. He started coming up the hallway banging on the walls, and saying "I want to go home"! He was carrying on like a reject. He went to his room and threw the bureau out, and the chair and saying "I want to go home."! The staff was like "what do we do"? The kid was looking at me, and the staff was looking at me. The kid wanted to kill me and the staff knew it. So they put all of us into the little room off the milieu and we had to wait for the staff to give us the all clear sign. Then the kid calmed down and, he was everybody's friend again, but I was still nervous. He got out and came back a week later. He was in the hallway sitting on a chair, and was noticeably troubled. The staff picked him up by the arms on each side of the kid, and dragged him down the hallway and threw him into his room.

One day I did the Lord's work by rebuking a chaplain. The guy had bushy bushy side burns. And he was Catholic. He started his 'sermon' in the tv room by talking about Sylvester Stallone, how he had a cliff lip and talked hoarsely. He went on by giving the "BODY OF CHRIST", in the wafer. I stood to him face to face and rebuked him like Paul telling Peter his error. I laid it on strong. I really let him have it about the errors of Catholism. But he went on and gave communion. I asked to see a wafer before everybody ate theirs and in so doing I made a girl think twice about the communion. I wanted to see the wafer to see what was on it. It passed inspection by me, but I didn't eat it. Later on in the food line, a guy came up to me and congratulated me for sticking up against that guy. I said "thank you".

One black counsilor, Benson, interviewed me. He sat down with me and he wanted to know my upbringing. He said "where did you grow up?" I said in PA. He asked me "what are your favorite sports teams.?" I said all the Philly teams. But he knew that before I said it. He somehow knew all about me before I told him anything.

Chapter 73

Bobby Mercury Again

One day I was in bed in my room. And I was dealing with God to kill me. I was trying to die, by God's hand. But I didn't die instead I was confronted by a gift from the Lord. I went out of my room into the milieu and there was Bobby Mercury. I went up to him and hugged him and said "Bobby Mercury"! We were happy to see each other. Bobby kept making referrals to the band Styrper, but I didn't want to talk about Stryper. I thought God wanted me to make Bobby mad enough at me that he would kill me.

So I followed Bobby around like a lost puppy dog and hoped Bobby would be mad enough to kill me. But I did the Lord's work by getting him to go to an AA meeting, and talk about his alcoholism, Bobby had no choice but to listen to the stories of the alcoholics, he went home a couple days later.

Chapter 74

The Laughing Fits

Each day was a new day to see what God would do through me. I spent each night waiting for the good things that would come my way the next day. I used to go to the milieu and just laugh my head off at everybody and everything.

My worker would bring me breakfast every morning to my room. But some days she forgot my fork on purpose, and I had to eat my eggs with my bare hand. She made me take a shower each day. And I had no choice but to get naked in front of her. She saw me naked all the time. And I thought I was going to have to walk naked all the time in front of everybody. She escorted me to the shower where I had to shower. She would stand outside at the door and tell me to get into the water. So I showered but had no clothes. I had to walk back to my room in a Johnny with my butt sticking out so everyone could see me. One day I pulled my pants down in the milieu in front of a guy. And I was naked in the room by bedroom. And Bobby Mercury saw me. Then I showed my nakedness to the social worker. I had no choice.

As I say each day was a laughing fit. I came out of my room one day and met a guy named Steven. I hugged him and I said" I love you Steven!" We threw a ball to each other in the milieu.

A girl there said she was having a heart attack and they said "well sit here." And they didn't do anything to help her. I thought it was funny and started laughing. Other girls were there who contended with me. She was saying "I like to drink tequila and eat the worm." She called me a diddler and she wanted to fight me. She threw insults at me and a package of crackers. I blocked the package with my outstretched hand; like Darth Vader blocking laser blasts from Han Solo. They were gonna attack me, this group of girls. But the staff stepped in and said "different people are here for different reasons", and they stopped.

One day I found a friend Bob, who gave me his Boston Red Sox hat. I stopped wearing my JESUS cap. I put on the headset one day and started rocking. Bob was laughing and saying "Go John!"

God put it on my heart to attack him so the next morning I went up to him and swung at his shoulder. I didn't hit hard just freaked him out a little bit. Later we played scrabble with impossible words that only God could make.

Chapter 75
The Blood Guy

The phlebotomist was the worst guy there. He wanted my blood at all the inopportunity's moments. He always talked about my class ring. Everybody talked about my class ring. The blood guy used to take my blood while I was talking to people. One day they took blood from me in my room, I complied with them but they said the next day I struggled with the nurse and scratched her which was total bullshit. They said I had AIDS, I said that's impossible. They just said it to mess with you. They once told me I was in Bay Ridge II and got assaulted. I was never in Bay Ridge II. They just try to mess with you to keep you off guard. They listen to your belly with the stethoscope over your clothes. They just pretend to be listening to your belly. One day a girl was crying in her room and the nurse just pulled the shade down on her door and left her crying in there. I hated that blood guy. He had tattoos on his arm. What phlebotomist has tattoos? I threw my ring in the trash, because it was the right thing to do at the time.

Chapter 76

The Room

Everyday it was the same routine as I lay in bed. The guy in the room next to me would use the bathroom. He shit 5x/day, and made me cringe. It felt like he was shitting on me. I knew his pattern, he would come in to drop something in the garbage, then he would come in and wash his hands. I knew his style all the way. But my room was like a sanctuary, no one could enter. Each day I lay in bed almost dead, and this annoying little councilor would egg me on to see the social worker. She kept saying "come on John?" She teased me into life.

I had to see the social worker everyday. She got me to admit that I don't like my father. But I do like my father. She kept asking me if I hear voices, which is kind of like a trick question, because I heard her voice, but she meant any audio hallucinations. I said no.

She kept bugging me with questions, and I just said yes, yes, yes, to each one. Then when I was finished with her I would go back to my room, and I had to listen to everybody's dilemma, as the social worker interviewed all the patients, I had to listen to everybody's speal. One day as I lay in bed, a doctor was questioni ng a girl, and was peppering her with psychological bullshit. She kept saying "I want to go home with my kids". And the doctor made her more uncomfortable. She kept on crying, and I couldn't take it anymore. I stormed out of my door, and said to the doctor," leave her the fuck alone, all she wants to do is see her kids, why can't you understand that?" And the doctor said "thank you very much for your opinion, Mr. Banner." And I got him to stop questioning her.

One day the guy in the next room was going to the bathroom on the toilet, and I had to go, so I peed in the trash bucket, while he was on the toilet. The mental health worker who brought my breakfast every morning, somehow found out and told me not to do it any more.

But every morning they would bring my breakfast into my room, and I caught them in their folly. The worker said "here is your breakfast." And I said "really now." And somehow I was able to turn over there dealings with me, and I was in control now.

One guy who bothered me a lot used to come in my room and quote the bible in a negative way. He always doomed me, but I saw his car in the parking lot out my window. He had a late model Volvo, but it had a rejection sticker on it. And I told the councilor to get him, because I wanted to kick his ass. I said "I want to kick his ass!" But he never came. One day in the outside walkway area, he saw my JESUS hat and said "I want to be a fucking Christian"! I almost said watch your tongue mister, but said nothing. Later I gave him my bible and my JESUS hat at the med window. I said here this is for you and he took it. Somehow before I went to the next hospital I got it back.

Chapter 77

In The Milleau

Everyday was a councilor named Wilfred. One day I came out of my room to start my day. I wondered why I didn't die that last night. And Wilfred showed me a picture of the human heart, and said this is why you are still alive, you can't kill the human heart. I cried.

But Wilfred was the main man, everything had to be dealt with by him. All problems, all questions, all dilemmas, had to go through him. I used to stand in the milieu as everyone walked around. There was this guy I called the opinion man, because he had a shaved head, and looked like an opinion man. I used to get out of everybody's way by walking around everybody. Wilfred helped me be a man. He was always pumping me up, getting me going be a man. One day he played "We Are The World" by 20 something pop/rock stars. I knew that song was bogus. He liked it but I downplayed it. He said "you can't put down another's music' but I did because that song is anti-God.

Then one day there was a guy who came in and had to have a security guard on him all the time. Wherever he went the security guard was with him. So I was kind of leary of this guy. One day we had a men's group with Mike. Mike was the group leader I always saw in the hallway but didn't go to any of his group until now. And at the group we started to talk about being a man. We saw a video about a guy who was comparing a man to a sports athlete. You have to win, you have to be a man. You've got to provide for your family. You've got to be a man. And this guy walks out with his security guard and left the room. That's one thing you don't do is leave a men's group in the middle of the group. He came back around 5 minutes later and said "I know I just left the group but I'm back now." So then naturally we started to talk about women, and Mike asked the question "What do you do with women?", and I said "you have to fuck them"! Everybody laughed. But then we talked about being able to support a family and being a family guy. But Mike sured up a belief in me that I had for along time is that women should neither smoke nor drink, because that wouldn't be very lady like. So anyways the group ended, and I told Mike "God bless you."

Another group was an art group, and we were told to write something down on paper, and I wrote "FUCK". Then they wanted us to show everybody what we wrote. I told them I don't want to share what I wrote with everybody, and said: I have no fucking talent anyways." And I left the group.

Another group I attended was an art group and I sat there and had no head. My head was not sitting on top of my neck. I was kind of invisible, and I sat there and had no head. I swear to God. So I left that group because I was embarrassed, and walked down the hall to the milieu, and I had no head walking down the hall, when I got to the kitchen table a miracle happened because on the table was Jimmy Swaggert's The Evangelist magazine. How could that get there except by God. I looked at it but I didn't pick it up to read and I was helped.

So one day after a group they had, there was a group schedule bulletin board. It had all the different groups and times they were started. And I was feeling kind of mean, and I erased all the times off the board, with the eraser. I felt like God wanted me to do this. Then I erased all the messages on the message board and wrote "FUCK U" on the board.

Chapter 78

The Food and the Lady with the Pill

Everyday at lunch and dinner the black guys would come with the food. It was or a rolling buffet cart. And it was so disgusting you wouldn't feed it to your dog. Everyday I ate just a salad and cereal. Sometimes they would make me grilled cheese or peanut butter and jelly sandwiches. But I requested cereal everyday and they gave it to me. I watched as the patients ate their food, and I said "How can you eat that?" I told everybody to eat cereal like me.

One day I was in line to get the food, when I was nervous about eating it, and the black guy tried to get me to eat the food like a dope dealer trying to sell pot. He's like "come on, come on." And I didn't eat. I stood there with every seat in the dining area was taken, the patients were all eating, and no one seemed to notice that I was just standing there looking on. The food was so disgusting.

One night as I lay in bed, I couldn't sleep, so I went to the med window to get something to help me sleep. I went to this lady and I told her I couldn't sleep. She holds out a pill and says "take it, take it." I was like "are you trying to kill me?" She said no, but insisted I take the medicine. God gave me a check on my left hand and I didn't take the pill. If I had taken that I would have been severely fucked up.

Chapter 79
My Visitors

So one day I was in the tv room and I came to my senses. I realized that I had been there 2 months, and I had better call my mom to get me out of here, or I would be here forever. I called my mother to see me and she came a couple times. She ate the disgusting food, but she couldn't see the monster I was. She would come and I wouldn't say anything or else on one occasion I complained on what goes on here.

Then my sister Cathy came to see me with my cousin Emily. Emily made me laugh. And Cathy told me to give her permission with all my financial situations. I had to write a leave of care to my sister. I didn't know what I was doing, I just singed away. She came a couple times to cheer me up. Then my fellow tenant from across the hall at my old apartment, Teri, came to see me, and she said "don't let them take your soul."

My mother came to see me one day, and I was talking to her at the table. This guy named Charlie was there and was interrupting me. So I said "I'm trying to talk to my mother" but it fell on deaf ears, and he kept talking. My mother was coaxing him on.

One kid there was only like 18. He had real skinny arms. He had a mentor who played monopoly with him. Charlie yelled to him one day "Hey dickhead"! We all laughed.

But I noticed Charlie was wearing my shirts. How did he get my shirts? I didn't bring them. How did he get them? Then this fat girl had my "Dinner On The Bridge" 2015 shirt on. And I was like how did she get my shirt? It was unbelievable.

Chapter 80

The Last Few Days

As I said before everyday was new and exciting at what God would do through me. I had the laughter fits. I would sit at the table and laugh at everybody and everything. I could tune into anyone's conversation even if they were on the other side of the room. This girl from Gloucester was there and I dug her. I did every thing towards her. I just followed her lead. She had a red neck friend from MA, but he spoke with a southern accent. He made me laugh all day long. I followed them as they walked around the outside walking area with the gazebo. I came up behind her and accidently stepped on her foot, then I almost grabbed her boob. I just followed her lead wherever she went.

One day I came out of my room and saw Benson the black councielor. I went up to him and said "Benson" and laid my head on his shoulder and laughed. I just laughed on his shoulder and laughed on his shoulder everywhere he went. I laughed with him all the way around on his "checks", I just laughed and laughed.

Then I laughed at my worker, the one who saw me naked. And we met another worker there and they made me laugh. The worker said "she's prettier than me." I had to laugh. They both started talking about their blonde hair and appearance, and it made me laugh.

One day a new girl came in with big boobs. And I told her about the Lord, saying JESUS is the only way to heaven. And I made her mad. So one night I came out of my room and came up to her and she was sitting at the councilor's table and I grabbed her tits and I said "JESUS LOVES YOU". Then I just left her there, and the staff said nothing.

Close to my last days there they showed me a video about ECT. It's a sleep thing where they put you under and you sleep. It's supposed to help severely depressed people. I didn't know that I would soon be doing ECT.

But one day they let us outside and we walked to the gazebo. And I spied a slogan written on top of the ceiling in the gazebo, it said "I Love You All." And I spied another slogan saying "You Are Not Alone". Then I spied a third slogan there but I forget what it said. Something positive.

One night we went out there and jet airliners were going by every 5 minutes. It was supernatural. The councilor pointed out to me the moon and next to it was she said "Venus". I thought that was pretty cool. But she said "you can see the ocean from here". I knew she was trying to play games with me. And I challenged her by saying "no you can't". And I wanted to bet her 5 bucks, but she didn't bet. I then told her about the bible how it says to avoid repetitious prayer. She marveled.

Chapter 81
The Round Up

I couldn't have a bowl movement for like 2 months. And I told Benson, I couldn't go. I got right up in Benson's face and yelled "I can't go"! And I was yelling and yelling and Wilfred said "John you can't get in Benson's face about this". And it made sense to me and I stopped yelling. But then Benson gave me an enigma in my room as John and another counselor looked on. But I was there lying on my side, and Benson started to give me the enigma. I screamed. He only gave me half the bottle then stopped. Then John said "John go there", but I was finally able to tell him no. So they all left me in the room.

One night I refused medications. When you refuse medications they give you an injection in the ass, because the medicine is court ordered. I came out of my room and started singing Pink Floyd's "Brick in the Wall". I sang "I don't need no medication! I don't need no thoughts control"! So I went to my room and 4 guys came in. And they were going to inject me. I started to take a swing at one guy and they overpowered me, and threw me on the bed, and pulled my pants down and shot me with a needle in the ass. They did this to me on two occasions. And it hurt. One night they came in my room and injected me with some shit in my elbow as I slept. Because I woke with a small patch on my elbow. They must have shot me during the night.

One day they gave me my belt back and I said "yeah there is a God". I was so happy to have my belt back.

Chapter 82

The Last Day

So the last day came and I played Battle Ship with the guy who left the men's group. He was so stupid, this game is for 10 year olds, to adults. And he couldn't figure it out. I taught a guy next to me how to play at the same time. I start out saying "all right, he's out there somewhere", and I call random shots. The guy couldn't even figure out how to play and I said "he's stupid".

So as I was saying my goodbyes to people because I was being taken to Layland unit in Beverly hospital, that I told Wilfred to make a man out of this guy. The guy who left the men's group. Then I said to John "find a conscionable job" then I said to the councilor again "Avoid repetitious prayer". I hugged everybody, wished everybody well, and they took me away on a stretcher. As I was in the ambulance on my way to Beverly I saw a sign in the courtyard "Bay Ridge Hospital". I saw it and gave it the middle finger. Then there was another sign that I saw as we drove by saying "Bay Ridge Hospital" I gave it the middle finger too as the EMT looked on. That was the end of Bay Ridge Hospital.

Chapter 83
Layland Unit Beverly Hospital

I arrived at Layland unit Beverly hospital by ambulance, carried in on a stretcher. I got off the stretcher and the first they do is strip search you. They escorted me to the restroom which is a unisex bathroom. And they make you take all your clothes off even your underwear. And two guys saw me naked. Then I was free to walk around the unit. I met a girl named Hilga, and I was told by her, that this is heaven. All the mental people in the world were the only ones to be saved. And the staff too because they were there to help you. And later I went back to my original idea, how its people saved by JESUS CHRIST. I looked out the window and saw a military helicopter, and I was scared, but the main man Dan said its alright. Then I asked him about the passage in the book of Revelation, chapter 13 about the beast and he said that's just religion trying to control you. But I later kept my first idea of the bible how its all true.

Then I met a nurse, Angela, who introduced me to the world of coloring. She gave me pictures of cows to color. I soon took to the new hobby. But then I saw Hilga again in the tv room and I grabbed her tit and masturbated right in front of her. I was half naked and the doctor, Doctor G, walked by. She didn't see my nakedness. Hilga didn't seem to care.

So they showed me to my room, I shared it with Charlie, an old man who helped me sleep at night, by his soft cooing.

That night I met Rick, another patient, who showed me how to make hot chocolate.

So in the morning a guy named Adolph, accused me of stealing his laundry. He yelled at me from down the hall. I was still in my room, so I came out to see what's he talking about. I said "how could I steal your clothes?, I just came out of my room just now." He apologized for accusing me.

Then we had art group with Suzan, a physical therapist. I colored pictures of mermaids, I soon had a whole stack of them. Adolph drew a self portrait of me and I put it with my mermaid pictures. Then someone stole the pile of pictures. But I went on undaunted coloring new pictures of mermaids. Then I did owls, angels, and fairies. Then I did dogs, birds, and flowers, over 200 pictures, that I still have with me today.

One day I got out of bed, and fell on my knees and elbows. My brain was freaking out. There was pressure in my head and it felt like my brain was spinning around. I somehow managed to get up and I went in the hall to tell staff for help. I almost went stark raving mad. The staff comforted me and I was able to function. That was the scariest moment in my life, I almost went totally insane.

Every morning Everett would come in and wake us up for breakfast. He was a cool dude. He would always sing a song to wake us up. Sometimes the staff would co me in and check Charlie, because he was always incontinent of urine and crap. They had to change his underwear. I got the heck out of there, that's the last thing you want to see, a senior citizen getting changed. Every morning at breakfast Ron would ask the group what they are going to do for the day. When it got to me it was the same thing everyday, I said "I'm going to color and play Risk".

While we were eating our breakfast, the staff would come with morning meds. They were injecting needles as patients were trying to eat their pancakes, and giving out pills where we eat.

Then there was a guy named Ralph. We knew each other from somewhere. But I used to go around with him as he made his rounds. I taught him how to play Acey duecy backgammon. We were like iron sharpens iron.

One day I was talking to Ralph about something, and one of the staff tried to listen. I caught him and told him to get the heck out of here.

Ralph told me where you hear the little bell go off, its another baby being born, as the maternity ward was right next door. One day a guy came in to stock the closet with stuff and I was with Ralph as he worked, and I just started laughing and laughing. One day with Ralph on his rounds, I kind of breathed and he said "that's a good thing to slow down like that.

Then there was Stan, Stan was the man, he was so cool. We played Battle Ship. Asked him "where are our missiles at?" He didn't know. Then I told him about common core, its a new way to teach children at school, how that the kid never has a wrong answer. If the kid puts down 2+2 equals 5, he's right. There is no more wrong answer. He told me its a waste of time to teach algebra because you never use it in the real world. He said they should teach kids how to balance your checkbook, and how to get a good credit score.

But I would always be in the tv room when Stan came in with the vital machine. He checked my vitals every day.

Chapter 84
The Patients

There was one guy there who's hair stuck out worse than an afro. It was so funny to look at, but he had constant gas, and he smelled like crap. I used to laugh at his hair, but then I felt sorry for him.

Then there was Tom. Tom was in a wheelchair, his bed was in my room. When he got up from his wheelchair he used to violently shake. His whole body was convolusing back and forth, he was shaking like a leaf on a tree, then he would just flop himself on the bed. I tried to help him by throwing a blanket on him and putting a pillow under his head. Tom had to be forced fed. He used to sit at the table as staff put food in his mouth. But Tom was smart, he knew exactly what was going on. You could see the wheels turn in his head. I was convinced that Tom was smarter then all of us, but didn't say it.

One day a black guy came to see Tom. Tom was in the kitchen and I sat at a table near him. The black guy came in and in super slow motion he fist pumped Tom. It was such an incredible act of love, I almost started crying. But Tom didn't belong in a psych hospital, he needed like a nursing home for his shakes. When he went to the bathroom he would clutch the wall and bang on the door for frustration. I felt so bad for him.

Another guy came in there who would never shut up. He used tossing all the songs out of key. I couldn't stand him. Thank God he was only there a week or two.

There was a girl there who was in a wheelchair also. I tried to talk to her but failed miserably. She was quite communicative and full of fun despite her handicap.

Then there was a guy who came in their that I met in Bay Ridge, and he used to piss me off because he only opened his eyelids halfway, so you could only see the bottom his eyes. He left soon.

Then there came in an old lady, and they put her bed outside by the nurses station. And she hollered all day long, yelling "I want to talk to my husband, fuck, shit, damn." "I want to talk to my husband, fuck, shit, damn."! And she yelled all day and all night. So finally I gave her a stuffed animal, and it quieted her right down, the staff looked on in amazement. She left soon.

Every day was almost the same. I would sit at the computer and look for apartments. One day as we all sat in the living room talking to Everette, Hilga spilt her coffee on me, I had to change clothes. But there was a disgusting social worker named Mark. He wore the same pants to work every day. He had a horrible laugh, just bellowing and disgusting. One of the patients mocked his laugh. I hope he got the message. He used to come in my room at night for checks, and he would always look at me first then the other two guys. At night they always watched Wheel of Fortune and Jeopardy. But he did help me make peanut butter and jelly sandwiches.

So each morning I had to see Dr. G. She was a Russian doctor. And I couldn't stand her. She opened the door to her office by kicking the door with her foot, her office smelled like b.o. And she wasn't going to let me go even if I was a straight A student. She kept saying "you have to stop crying" I sued to cry at night but how did she know that. I showed her all my coloring pages and held up the game board to Castle Risk which has the Russian empire on it I tried to score brownie points with her.

One day I had another attack in my mind. I was delirious and out of control. I came in the hallway outside my room and started yelling "Cathy, Cathy." My sister's name. I rolled on the floor in a seizure. And the doctor G. was there along with a couple nurses and workers. And I yelled to the doctor "I want to fuck you"! And they tried to restrain me. They wrapped me up in like a blanket and carried me to a quiet room, and they laid me on a table. I rolled off of it and fell to the floor. They picked me back up again and put me back on the table. There were 3 men to my side and one farted, I said "Fuck You"! Then they pulled my pants down and shot me in the ass with a needle of Haldol. After about 10 minutes they all left the room except one guy. I started to come out of it, and began talking to the guy. I told him he was a good guy. But Frederick was an asshole. He was a mean councilor. But the councilor got nervous because I was seeing with my eyes, him. And he said "what are you doing now?" And I just said "I am calming down." So that was a horrible episode and the doctor didn't hold it against me for what I said.

There was a nice nurse there named Cynthia. She was attractive and just slightly overweight. She used to dance with the male patients. One guy was dancing with her and was looking at her breasts the whole time. She didn't seem to mind and when they were done dancing the guy yells out "now dance with this guy, meaning me. So I danced with her for a minute and she wanted me to twirl, but I said "you twirl", and she did. She always gave me morning meds at breakfast time, you don't want to swallow pills when your eating your eggs.

Then they had a guitarist come in and she would sing pop songs as the patients would all sing along. It struck a nerve with me and I couldn't stand the singing. So I had to go to my room to avoid hearing.

But art group was a lot of fun. Suzan would have us all in the art room, and I colored as the music was playing. I then made a necklace of beads, which I wear to this day to remind me of my stay in the hospital. One guy looked at my coloring and said nice,". I took the compliment. And Suzan would take us outside to the patio. Its just a small outdoor area with about 10 chairs. We used to sit out there and talk and play trivia.

But Angela the nurse who introduced me to coloring also started an art group in the evening. It was way more fun and laid back then Suzan's group. We all did arts and crafts, I colored listening to the radio. I used to get my drawings of coloring pages from like 6, 3 ring notebooks, I did it myself, just grabbing the pictures I wanted to color.

There was this other woman there who made me laugh all the time. When a song came on the radio she always knew it and sang along to it. She knew all the songs and I just laughed with her and laughed with her.

Then a woman came in and I sat beside her at breakfast. But then I realized her problem, she never shut up. She went on and on about every subject under the sun and would not stop talking. But she was deaf and had to have her family bring in her hearing aid. Her family came and tried to talk to her, but they couldn't get word in edge wise. She would not stop talking. One day she fell in the shower and had to go to the ER. She had a black and blue spot over her eye.

Then I met a girl and she became my special friend. She was small but cute, and we sat together at meals and played Backgammon and Risk. When she left the unit she kissed me and I wanted to call her on the phone at her house, but then I lost the number and never made contact again.

One of the nurses I didn't like was so stupid. I laid in bed one night and couldn't get up out of bed. So she's talking to me I couldn't talk or wouldn't talk. And she says to me "if you can understand me blink twice." I thought that was so stupid, I wasn't about to do that. One night she gave me my meds, and said "are you ready for your meds?" I said "sure". And a male nurse got turned on or something because I said that. A couple nights later we talked sports in the kitchen.

One night a lady patient needed medical attention. Some EMT's came into the unit, and attended to her. They got an eyeful as they had never been in the unit before. The whole Beverly hospital has no idea what goes on in the Layland unit. No one does. That's the reason for this book, so the world may know what goes on behind these closed doors.

Then they had a machine in my room to lift people out of bed. They were using it on Charlie, and I came in to the room and saw this behemoth apparatus and said "what the fuck is that?" They explained its to lift Charlie out of bed, so they don't hurt their backs.

Finally with about a week to go they put me in another room. This was a much nicer room with one roommate. I got along fine with him without speaking to him.

I got to talk to a councilor and he interviewed me and basically we got the answer of what my problem is "I don't know". And I had conversations with Everette, and Ralph, and Stan. I told Everette a couple stories and he said I should write a book, which is another reason I wrote this book. I played Backgammon with Ralph and the other counsilor from the quiet room. Backgammon is so cool, we used to play it in high school and I remembered how to play it all these years later. I introduced it to them and they loved it. I used to play and beat Stan at Battle Ship.

One night a councilor came in my room and sat on the side of my bed. He started asking questions, and I put my foot on his stomach and was about to push him off. He said "don't do that" I said "get the fuck out of here" and he left.

So with just a couple days I left they told me I was going to Tewksbury State hospital, and I was down. I said "I'll never make it there", because I visited my uncle Jack there once and knew it was a hard place.

But Ralph told me I would be alright. They had horses there and computers.

So I hugged Cynthia and Angela and said goodbye to everyone and they put me on a stretcher and took me by ambulance to Tewksbury State Hospital.

Chapter 85
Tewksbury State Hospital

When I arrived at Tewksbury state, they dropped me off the stretcher and brought me into a little nurses room they checked my extremities, my hands and my feet. They asked me questions and told me about life at the hospital. So they showed me my room in the middle of the hall, but then I got a better room, at the end of the hall. And I saw my doctor for the first time. She was so loving and caring and so sweet. She asked me what's my diagnosis, and I said I have psychophrenia. That slipped out, she would have found out anyway, but that gave her so much power over me. I told her the next day that I didn't mean to say that. But I got introduced to my roommates. One kid around 20, one Chinese kid the same age, one guy in the middle, and one dickhead on the opposite side of me.

I was still realing from the admission of psychophrenia to the doctor, that I opened up to the 20 year kid and wanted to make the best of it by starting a conversation. He asked me if I was religious. I guess it shows, and I said "yes". He told me about the dickhead guy who always played his rock "music" at night real loud. I said there is no way he's gonna play music at night when I am trying to sleep. This guy was always flashing me the devil sign with his fingers. And I used to flash the peace sign at him.

They had a big room where we all would eat. I sat with the kid at every meal. I couldn't have made it without him. We used to sit at opposite sides of each other and bounce man to man with him. The food was disgusting here too, except for the tator tots, and cookies. I used to just eat cereal here too.

Every morning after breakfast you would have to take your meds. There was always a line. We always went back to bed after that. The Japanese kid all he did was eat and sleep, eat and sleep. So I played Backgammon with the kid, and he said it was boring, and didn't want to play Castle Risk either.

But there were 2 tv rooms and we would always sit in the one and watch football. One day we were watching football and this black guy comes in and he sat down behind us. And he started singing some Spanish song and crying. We both yelled at him to stop but he kept on.

So one day they promised to show me these mysterious horses. I went out with the councilor Jeff, and another patient, and the horse worker girl. We walked to the paddock area and petted and fed the horse with handfuls of grass. I wanted to ride them but they said we could only feed and pet them at this time. So I was only half way thrilled with these horses.

But they also promised me I could cook. But they never took me to the kitchen but they always allowed me to go to the computer room, as I was on full privileges. I took the elevator to the first floor, and went on line looking for apartments. I saw many and visited a couple apartments with my mother.

One day the doctor who always meets with me in the morning took me out for a walk around the campus. She showed me how to look around myself and see all the sights and wonders, the flowers, and birds, chipmunks, and squirrels. All the things I never would have noticed before now I see everything clearly. One day in a group meeting with my doctor, Doctor H, and another doctor, and a nurse and a councilor with me, and I just broke down crying. Everybody was touched. But at number of meetings, with the group, they determined my future, and the deal was that if I could find an apartment I could go, or be forced to go to a respite house. Which is kind of like a group home. So that was my goal, find an apartment.

One kid said he was there for four years. I said "you deserve a merit button." Another guy who was a big guy, used to scare me. He used to walk around with his left arm sticking out his side. He was going to kill me or beat me badly. I steared clear of him. Later he kind of buddied up to me but I was still leary. There was a black guy who always asked me for money. I think I gave him a buck.

One day I was in my room feeling down. And the dickhead guy told me a derogatory remark that made me feel downer still. So I got off my bed and approached him and took a big swing at him. He blocked it, but I threw another one at him, but I pulled the punch stopping just short for his eye. Because I really didn't want to fight. I left the punch there just to show him what could happen. But each night he played his "music" in bed. We made him wear head phones at night. He kept flashing me the devil horn sign at me with his fingers, and I would always flash the peace sign with my fingers.

Each morning Dr. H. would come to see me. She met me at my door and gave me couple minutes to get myself together. Then we would meet. She was so kind and gentle, I wanted to walk with her each day outside, but she couldn't. I kept telling her I want my peanut butter and jelly sandwiches for supper. Once in a while I had to meet with my whole treatment team. That is nervous for me because its like a jury of your peers, judge you. But each time they kept telling me "you're doing good keep it up."

Every day was the same thing. This black girl with stupid hair would start yelling and screaming. She kept on about her human rights. But she would scream and swear, and scream and swear. They had to call the police and security. Always over the loud speaker "Code Grey Delta Five, Code Grey Delta Five". That meant for the cops and security to come.

Another day a new black girl came in, a teenager. She was very petite, and very cute. But with a mouth that would match any swearing sailor on the sea. She wouldn't shut up, swearing and yelling, just filthy communications out of her mouth. They had to call "code grey" on her all the time too. She would especially swear in the dining room. You're trying to eat your meal, when you've got this young teenager swearing like a sailor all through dinner.

But they had student nurses who came to see us. I played Backgammon with a couple of them. Then they would hold craft night, and I colored a pumpkin and put stickers on it. All the while trying to avoid the guy who wanted to kill me. I had to avoid him like the plague.

Chapter 86
Wrapping Tewksbury State Hospital

My father came to see me and we went to Gloucester to look at apartments. I met his new wife for the first time. She is sweet and deaf too. So then we saw a couple of apartments and went to the Azorian restaurant. My father made me put in $10 for my meal. Then he brought me back to the hospital.

One day me and the dickhead guy were in the room together, and I played Bride on my boom box, and the guy was impressed by them. And I played a couple songs for him and he said he would get Bride tapes too. So I made friends with the guy.

Then there was this guy who I saw always walking down the hallways. And I thought he was a smooth character. And I knew if I asked him to play Risk he would. So I asked him to play and I was right he did. We played one game and I won. Then I asked him if he wanted to play again and he said "no". But I got him to play the next day and we did and I won again.

So the day I left was like a whirlwind. I had to meet the social worker and the nurses. And finally a normal human being gave me a ride out of there. But before I left I gave all my change around $1.50 to the black guy who bummed from me, and made his day. But one more thing about black people. I never had so many African Americans ask me what my name is. And some of them were so stupid I had to point out my name on their checklist.

The last thing I want to say about name Tewksbury is that when they come to your door at your room at night and do checks, and shine flashlight at each of us, it doesn't matter. It's not real, it's just a game.

So I left Tewksbury State Hospital with the lady, and she drove me to my new home, a respite house in Danvers.

So all together for trying to kill myself I spent 7 months in 3 different hospitals. 52 was the worst year of my life.

Chapter 87

The Respite House

When I first got to the respite house in Danvers, I was introduced to all the patients. Hilda was there from Layland unit so I had a friend. They showed me my room. I had to share it with a roommate, Omar, who snored at night. It was very awful. But they gave me a demonstration of what to do in a fire. They showed me how to run downstairs, from the third floor out the side door to the tree. They had a mock fire drill at least twice while I was there.

They wake you up in the middle of the night, and the alarm sounds very loudly. You are trying to sleep and the alarm goes off and you have to run outside and meet by the tree across the street.

Omar used to get under my skin watching tv. He kept saying "right John, right John". And I had to say, right.

One guy said he was Wiccan, and he shot heroin for like 6 years. And Justin was there, I remember him from Bay Ridge, though I did not say to him, "I know you" to him.

Then a kid named Sam came in. We made fast friends. We were always talking sports to each other, baseball, basketball, football, and hockey. Justin used to like the show "My 600lb life". I used to laugh and laugh at the fatso's. A worker there Tom, with green hair, who used to just sit on the couch with his laptop, kinda scolded me about laughing at them, and I said "they shouldn't have put so much food in their mouths".

Then we watched Live PD., and the cops and suspects, made me laugh and laugh. Chris who came in later, who I recognized from Bay Ridge, said "its good to hear you laughing."

One guy came in there who I didn't like at all, because he was mean looking. I gave him strong witness about the Lord. Thank God he left soon.

Another guy came in there with a beard and looked gruff. He shaved it off the next day, and you would hardly know he was a nice guy clean shaven. He would always eat his supper at the end of the table. He used to let me listen to music choice on tv and once in a while I would put it on the classic station. We listened to all the famous classics.

So it was great, just me, Sam, Justin, Ted, and Jennifer, and Sarah. We all got along, we all had fun, watching sports on tv, and playing Risk and Scrabble. Then one day a new girl came in there named Sheana, and another guy, Aarron. And they took over the tv watching movies all day and all night. Me and Sam couldn't watch any sports at all. So we complained to Phil, the director of the house, and he made a rule that everybody gets 1 hr. on the tv.

Every morning they would wake you up around 7 am to get meds. I used to take mine and get the Boston Globe every morning, because I had it delivered. Then I went back to bed til around 12:00 or 1:00. Sam had a hard time getting up in the morning. They had to wake him up two or three times to get meds. Some mornings they would have group. It was so stupid, you had to go to group or leave the house for an hour. So I went to group. A black lady ran it, but she had poor English that was hard to understand. And Tom would listen to the group seated at his desk in the staff's med and nursing room. I told her to close the door so Tom couldn't hear. We asked him but he refused to close the door. Everyone took turns reading from a piece of paper, and talking about psych issues. The readings were so stupid, they made no sense.

So every day or so me and Sam would walk to the Dunkin Donuts and CVS. I frequented the toy store. They played board games on Sundays and Tuesdays. They had real cool games there but very expensive, around $50 or $70/games so I never bought one. Then I used to go to the plant store and I bought a couple plants and brought them to the house. Then I used to go to Danvers coin and shop for cd's and tapes. It became my favorite store. Then I would go to CVS and buy newspapers and cereal. I used to cut out cool pictures from the paper and send them to my nephew Seamus, in KY to start a scrap book. He did a few but wasn't interested in keep on doing it.

One day me and Sam went to the Osbourne's pub. I had a beer and Sam had a beer and a whiskey. I was kind of wondering if I should be in that bar. But I looked at my dollar bill and saw the motto "IN GOD WE TRUST", so I took it that God was with me. But while sitting there drinking a beer the tv and liquor bottles began being evil. So we left there and I had a small buzz. But I could tell it was messing with my medications. And when we got home a new girl was there Holly. I kinda blew my witness because I was buzzing when I met her. I went to my room and at everything the evil passed away. Thank God.

Chapter 88
The Staff

The staff at respite house was mainly black people. One black guy Gus was cool. He gave me my meds sometimes at night. He used to wear African clothing. Another black guy in the morning was cool. He helped me get my paper every morning, after meds were passed out. But the one black woman Valeri was like a Nazi captain. She barked orders around the kitchen, "wash dishes,! who's mess is this?" She used to put toothpaste on her hands and pass out medicine. I said "you are not going to give me my meds with toothpaste hands"! So she washed her hands, but then she used to pass out meds in her bare feet. Her and Gus used to talk back and forth with each other in mumbo jumbo, voodoo gutter trash talk. It was painful to listen to because we were trying to watch tv. but these 2 black people were jawing at each other. I saw Gus asleep at his desk like 14x and Valeri would cover for him saying "he's tired."

But one guy there was cool, Ed. I used to try to get him to play Strattego. But he kept saying "I can't now." Then they used to drive me to get my blood work done. It always interrupted my whole day and sleep patterns. Then one day they took me to Lynn to see my thyroid doctor. I always prayed for help from God before I left with them. I prayed to God before I did anything everytime, still do. I don't do anything without praying to God first and he always hears me and helps me.

Sometimes at night I would cry to JESUS, and my roommate Justin said "yes my son." It made me feel bad. But I always cried to JESUS all the time.

Chapter 89

The Clients

So me and Justin would play Castle Risk, and me and Sam would play scrabble. I played scrabble with Sheana, I too, and her friend who was visiting. Aarron was there too, he was a fat slob, who always had his pants halfway down his ass, and his crack showed. It used to piss me off, but once you get to know him he's alright.

One night we were having a group meeting when Sheana turned blue, stopped breathing and passed out. Everyone yelled out "call 911! Call 911!. Staff took their time and finally called. The EMT's arrived, the police and the firemen all came. They gave Sheana narcon, because she was overdosing on opioids. They said if they got there 5 minutes later she would have been dead. So she awoke, and they took her to the hospital for evaluation. Needless to say she gave us all a fright.

The guy named Ted he was quiet as a mouse, and Holly the new girl used to come in my room and steal me and Justin's change. We told Phil the director but he did nothing about it.

Chapter 90

Leaving the House

Phil used to bring his dog to the house, and that was cool, Phil also played the guitar for everyone but I didn't like his music so I left the room. He had a mean side to. He was bald and with a goatee. He would condescend on the patients standing on the side of their problems...so the staff could see him trying to be good to people. He was a nice guy but needs help with his bed side manner.

So finally I got my apartment at the Heights at Cape Ann, in W. Glouc., and I left the house. I packed up all my belongings the night before and I had like 6 garbage bags full of clothes, and papers, and games, and stuff. So the next day my mother came and picked me up and Sam helped me carry my stuff to the car. I had the car packed to the gills, but I forgot my plants, so we had to come back the next day to get the plants. But a nurse from able home care followed us to the heights and gave me my medicine. So then it was all over.

So I did 5 months at the respite house, and 7 months in 3 different hospitals.

So I say to you dear reader, if you're contemplating suicide don't do it, because you'll only go to a psych hospital, sentenced by a judge you will not see to do 6 months there and possibly more by the time its all said and done. So if you can't do the time don't do the crime.

God Bless You and remember "God has not given us a spirit of fear, but of power, love, and of a sound mind.!

THE END

About the Author

John Banner was born in Laredo, TX, 9/29/66, to military parents. Both were in the Air Force. His father was a jet fighter pilot, while his mother was an RN. When the parents tour of duty was over, we moved to Gloucester, MA; where John's brother Chris was born. Then the family moved to New York, where John went to preschool, and kindergarten. Then the family moved to New Jersey where John's sister Cathy was born. Then the family moved to Pennsylvania, there in the rolling hills of Pennsylvania the family raised horses, cows, goats, pigs, chickens, and sheep on a farm.

John's father was an airline pilot for TWA, so the family enjoyed many glorious traveling experiences abroad.

Then tragedy struck the family as his parents got divorced. John and his father travelled to Kentucky, while his brother, sister, and mother moved to Gloucester, Massachusetts.

John finished high school on Kentucky, then moved to Gloucester to be with his mother and siblings.

After living in Gloucester for formal years, John experienced psychological problems, and had to be hospitalized on many occasions.

John lived with alcohol, and drug addiction, with marijuana being his drug of choice.

Sadly tragedy struck again as John's brother Chris died of a rare disease in Seattle, WA.

One day John found Jesus as his personal Lord, and Saviour, or should I say Jesus found him, as John was born again. John lived a Godly lifestyle though still had mental problems, and drug dependency. This day John is clean from drugs and alcohol, though still takes medicine for mental health issues.

John had an apartment with a fort as for view of Gloucester Inner Harbor, Gloucester is a city rich in seafaring history, and delicious seafood.

One day, John tried to commit suicide, because his illness was too much for him, and he had to be committed to three different psych hospitals for 7 months. Then he was committed to a halfway house for 5 months. So John lost his entire 52nd years.

But today, John's devoted to his church, and is an avid sports fan. John is a cancer survivor, from having thyroid cancer, both of them, and skin cancer, and most??? neck cancer.

Today, John live in a nice apartment in W. Gloucester, with a cat and a hamster.

Printed in the United States
By Bookmasters